The Social Application of Religion

By

CHARLES STELZLE, JANE ADDAMS,
CHARLES P. NEILL, GRAHAM
TAYLOR, AND GEORGE
P. ECKMAN

THE MERRICK LECTURES FOR 1907–8

Delivered at Ohio Wesleyan University, Dela-
ware, Ohio, April 5–9, 1908

I0083053

WIPF & STOCK · Eugene, Oregon

Wipf and Stock Publishers
199 W 8th Ave, Suite 3
Eugene, OR 97401

The Social Application of Religion
By Stelzle, Charles, Addams, Jane, Neill, Charles P.,
Taylor, Graham, and Eckman, George P.
ISBN 13: 978-1-60608-136-5
Publication date 11/19/2008
Previously published by Jennings and Graham, 1908

THE MERRICK LECTURES

By the gift of the late Frederick Merrick, M. D., D. D., LL. D., for fifty-one years a member of the Faculty, and for thirteen of those years President of Ohio Wesleyan University, a fund was established providing an annual income for the purpose of securing lectures within the general field of Experimental and Practical Religion. The following courses have previously been given on this foundation:

Daniel Curry, D. D.—"Christian Education."

President James McCosh, D. D., LL. D.—"Tests of the Various Kinds of Truth."

Bishop Randolph S. Foster, D. D., LL. D.—"The Philosophy of Christian Experience."

Professor James Stalker, D. D.—"The Preacher and His Models."

John W. Butler, D. D.—"Mission Work in Mexico."

Professor George Adam Smith, D. D., LL. D.— "Christ in the Old Testament."

Bishop James W. Bashford, Ph. D., D. D., LL. D.—"The Science of Religion."

James M. Buckley, D. D., LL. D.—"The Natural and Spiritual Orders and Their Relations."

John R. Mott, M. A., F. R. G. S.—"The Pastor and Modern Missions."

Bishop Elijah E. Hoss, D. D., LL. D.; Professor Doremus A. Hayes, Ph. D., S. T. D., LL. D.; Charles E. Jefferson, D. D., LL. D.; Bishop William F. McDowell, D. D., LL. D.; Bishop Edwin H. Hughes, D. D., LL. D.—"The New Age and Its Creed."

Robert E. Speer, M. A.—"The Marks of a Man; or, The Essentials of Christian Character."

INTRODUCTION

No OTHER series of the Merrick Lectures ever attracted so large audiences as the lectures now published—the twelfth course on this foundation.

In great part this was due to the fame of the speakers. Most of them are of more than national reputation. Their commanding personalities, their varied talents, their wide experience, and their eminent usefulness in differing positions inevitably drew large numbers, anxious to hear people who had done things tell what things ought to be done—and why. Though the lecturers represent several religious denominations, and have been looking at different aspects of the social situation, and gave their addresses without previous consultation with one another, the general agreement of their views is striking.

In part also, the interest in the lectures arose, as I believe, from the topics which they discussed. There is a genuine social awakening—a deepening, if not new, sense of universal responsibility—which has shown itself in philanthropy, in political reform, in vigorous discussion of family problems and commercial morality, in ardent and not unsuccessful efforts for industrial and social betterment. The cru-

sade of our day, which kindles the noblest ambitions
of many high souls, is a social crusade. Knowledge
of surrounding needs, clearer than ever before; the
humanizing of religion, the exaltation of Jesus as
Teacher and Example,—all have tended to enlarge
the ranks of social workers, to put Christian com-
passion into practice.

For this awakening, no doubt, the Church is
largely responsible. Certain it is that, for her own
sake and for the work's sake, she must be closely
identified with it. The age will suffer, civilization
will languish, if evangelism and social service, which
are but parts of one enterprise, should be brought into
opposition or should even be separated. The Church,
if she is to retain the confidence of the people, must
be the servant of the people with their multitudinous
needs. She must not only preach love, but prove
love by a service that seeks no return. She must
not only preach courage, but be bold in her attitude
toward those who are strong and cruel. She must
offer faith, and she must also have faith enough to
stake her very existence on the ultimate triumph
and the present supremacy of righteousness and
peace. If the wreck of our civilization is to be
averted, the Church must be the champion of the
weak.

Likewise, for greatest sanity, efficiency, and permanence of results, the self-sacrificing social workers
of our day should be living and laboring under the
restraints and guidance and inspirations of religion.

Some are in religious perplexity. Their very service of love should bring fuller knowledge of divine things. In the following of Christ, they may learn more of the pre-eminence of the Lord and Savior of men. Willing to do His will, they may know of the doctrine.

In Jesus Christ is the hope of society as well as of individuals. Those who worship Him and those who serve Him should be at one to put Him on the world's throne.

As the Church wisely joins herself with all who seek to make this earth a better dwelling for the children of God, she will not lose evangelistic fervor, forget her missionary responsibilities, or neglect her educational institutions. All, in happy harmony, shall evidence the breadth of her mission and the sincerity of her love.

HERBERT WELCH.

Ohio Wesleyan University.

CONTENTS

I

THE SPIRIT OF SOCIAL UNREST

CHARLES STELZLE,

Superintendent of the Departments of Church and Labor
and of Immigration of the Board of Home Missions of the Presbyterian Church in the
United States of America.

I

THE SPIRIT OF SOCIAL UNREST

TWENTY-FIVE years ago a famous French statesman said, "The social question is a fad upon which serious statesmen should waste no time." To-day no thinking man will deny that it is the most important question that confronts us. This is true largely because our leaders in Church and school and State have persistently closed their eyes to the signs of the times. The awakening interest in recent years has come none too soon. For already the horizon is dark with clouds of social unrest which may distill into blessed showers or break upon us in a storm of fury.

Nowhere is this truer than in our great centers of population. Like a great whirlpool, the city draws unto itself the elements which constitute the social unrest. The growth of the city is one of the wonders of modern times. We are accustomed to speak of the growth of cities only in connection with the development of our own new country, but this is a world phenomenon. The same elements which make the city here make it across the sea. The city is the-product of the newer civilization. It is the outgrowth of modern economic and social conditions from which there is no turning back. Therefore the city will unquestionably dominate the nation. Whereas in 1800 only four per cent of the population of the United States lived in the city, to-day thirty-four per cent live in the town. Whereas in 1800 there were only six cities with a population of 8,000 in America, to-day there are six hundred such cities. In these cities there are found more than twenty-five million people. From 1890 to 1900 the total increase of population in the United States .was twenty per cent. But during the same period the population of the cities increased thirty-seven per cent.

The factors which are developing the city will never disappear. The introduction of labor-saving machinery multiplies the efficiency of those who remain on the farm, but it fails to increase the eating capacity of the rest of the world. It is quite evident that with the decreased demand for manual labor on account of the use of machinery, the farmer is driven to the city where he can find employment in shops where not only agricultural implements are turned out, but every other conceivable object, for which the demands are almost unlimited. Notwithstanding the attempts of well-intentioned philanthropists to induce immigrants and other classes to move onto the land, these immigrants and working people persist in remaining in the city, not only for the reasons already given, but because while

the country-bred man driven into the city finds it
comparatively easy to adapt himself to city life, the
city-bred man rarely adjusts himself to the ways
of the country. Those who do go to the country
are the ones who are comparatively free from the
very thing that seems to make this step necessary.
With the rapidly developing transportation facilities,
the business man who makes his money in the city
can easily make his home in the suburb. And
usually he assumes no responsibility for the city's
civic and religious life, often leaving it in the hands
of the most unfit. Because of these changing conditions, and because in the cities are found every
element which has tested the strength and the
virility of the Church, and in some instances destroyed the very life of government which had given
promise of permanence, it is not difficult to understand that we are facing forces which challenge
us for supremacy in the great storm centers of population.

Furthermore, I would remind you that the city
is peculiarly an industrial problem. The economic
interpretation of history seems to explain the long
series of events which have followed one another in
the development of mankind. Other influences there
have been which can not be catalogued under this
study, but nevertheless the fundamental basis of the
development has been economic and industrial. It
has been pointed out that the life of primitive man
was largely determined by certain economic factors

--the discovery of fire, the invention of pottery, the domestication of animals, and the use of tools. We assign industrial names to the ages, as, the age of stone, the age of brass, the age of bronze, and the age of iron. We talk of the hunting and fishing, the pastoral and agricultural, the commercial and industrial stages of civilization. The early migrations, the abolition of slavery, the awakening of nations, the American and French Revolutions, and most of the wars of history were largely due to economic causes. There is to-day no great political question before the American people which is free from the economic factor. Nearly every law passed by the legislature, and nearly every governmental enterprise, has its economic aspect, if indeed it is not altogether economic in its nature.

But it is the human element in the city's life which must chiefly concern us. The filthy slum, the dark tenement, the unsanitary factory, the long hours of toil, the lack of a living wage, the back-breaking labor, the inability to pay doctors' bills in times of sickness, the poor and insufficient food, the lack of leisure, the swift approach of old age, the dismal future,—these weigh down the hearts and lives of multitudes in our cities. Many have almost forgotten how to smile. To laugh is a lost art. The look of care has come so often and for so long a period at a time that it is now forever stamped upon their faces. The lines are deep and hard; their souls —their ethical souls—are all but lost. No hell in the future can be worse to them than the hell in which they now live. They fear death less than they fear sleep. Some indeed long for the summons, daring not to take their own lives.

To such what does it matter whether the doors of the Church are closed or open? What attraction has the flowery sermon or the polished oration? What meaning have the Fatherhood of God and the brotherhood of man? Where is God? they ask; and What cares man? they say. It is in meeting the needs of these that the Church will be severely tested in coming days.

Closely allied to this element of city life is the problem and challenge of the immigrant. He is coming at the rate of a million a year. Always will he continue to be amongst us. True enough, many of them are going back in these days of business depression, but they are going back as missionaries to tell of the glories of this great country, and every one that has gone back will bring a dozen with him. So long as there is a pull on this side of the ocean and a push on the other, and the push is constantly becoming harder, millions of foreigners, with their distorted views of government, will continue to come. To many of these the word government means oppression. They land on the American shore with a hatred and malice in their hearts which only too frequently finds expression in the use of the pistol and bomb. Anyway, this swelling tide of immigra-

2

tion adds greatly to the spirit of social unrest in our country.

The problem of the immigrant is peculiarly an American one. Only about eight per cent of the population of Paris are foreign born. London has less than three per cent foreign born. But, according to the census of the United States in 1900, the one hundred and sixty cities having at least twenty-five thousand inhabitants have a foreign born population of more than twenty-six per cent. It is worthy of attention that the six cities having the largest percentage of foreign born inhabitants are in Massachusetts. Fall River has forty-seven per cent; Lawrence, forty-five per cent; Lowell, forty-three per cent; Holyoke, forty-one per cent, foreign born. These New England cities exceed Chicago with its thirty-four per cent, and New York with its thirty-five per cent. In history the immigrant has conquered nations; not always by force of arms, but by method of life or by force of character. Sometimes for good; often for ill. The average immigrant will make a good citizen if the American will show him how. And the American citizen has more to do with the solution of the problem than has the immigrant himself.

Another element which must be included in the discussion of this subject is organized labor. Affiliated with the American Federation of Labor there are one hundred and seventeen international organizations, thirty-nine State organizations, five hundred

and eighty-five central labor unions, composed of the
labor unions of particular cities and counties, and
twenty-eight thousand local organizations. Add to
these the great railroad brotherhoods, the Industrial
Workers of the World, and still other smaller organizations, and you have a total of three and one-
half millions. It has been said that the workingmen in the labor organizations represent but a small
part of the great mass of toilers. The census of
1900 tells us there were in this country at that time
twenty-nine million persons engaged in gainful occupations. But we must eliminate from our calcu-
lation the ten million farmers who are unorganizable.
We must eliminate nearly all of the six million persons in social and domestic service who are not yet
in labor unions, fortunately or otherwise. We must
eliminate the million and a quarter persons in pro-
fessional practice. All of these are unorganizable
and should be excluded from the comparison. Eliminate also large numbers of the nearly five millions
in trades and transportation, which includes bankers
and brokers, the officials of banks and corporations,
bookkeepers, overseers, hucksters, stenographers, ped-
dlers, undertakers, and a long list of people who can
not be organized into labor unions. After you have
taken out these, you have just about seven millions
left. Probably one-half of them are living in small
towns where there are no labor unions, or else they
are engaged in occupations which have not yet been
or can not be organized. So that practically the

three and one-half millions in the labor unions really represent the great mass of artisans and laborers in our country. And when they speak, they speak officially for the working people of the United States.

I said a moment ago that the farmers were not yet included in the ranks of organized labor. It was most interesting, during the last two conventions of the American Federation of Labor, to witness that strong group of men representing a newly organized farmers' society which threatens to sweep the entire country. These dozen men asked to be received as delegates to the American Federation of Labor. They pledged their organization to a hearty co-operation in the things for which organized labor stands. If a complete union between these organizations is consummated, it will mean the practical co-operation of the wage-earning and agricultural interests of the United States, and if this should ever take place it will undoubtedly very radically affect the social and economic conditions of the masses.

But, more significant than any other element in the discussion of this subject is that of Socialism. There are to-day twenty-five million Socialists throughout the world; as many people as there are in every city of the United States with a population of eight thousand and over. Eight millions of them have already cast their ballots for Socialist candidates.

Last August, in the city of Stuttgart, Germany, the Socialists held their international congress, with

eight hundred and eighty-six delegates coming from
twenty-five different countries. On the first Sunday
afternoon of that great convention they had a mass-
meeting of one hundred thousand working-people in
the Plaza of Stuttgart. From the surrounding towns
and from Stuttgart itself, there came never-ending
processions of Socialists, until they surrounded the
six stands from which the speakers gave their addresses. The police, sent out to quell riots, were
engaged simply in ministering to those who had
fainted by the wayside on account of the oppressive-
ness of the day. It seemed very much like the day
of Pentecost, as those half-dozen men spoke in different languages. Sometimes those gathered before
them were unable to understand the words which
they were speaking, but they could catch the spirit
which was back of them, and they were thrilled by
the messages which meant so much to them,—this
great human brotherhood of Socialists, which is making such tremendous progress throughout the entire
world.

If the Socialists in our own country increase in
the same ratio during the next eight years as they
increased during the four years preceding the last
Presidential election, they will elect a President of
the United States. Some time ago I was talking in
a Western college. I invited questions from the
audience. The most pointed questions that were put
at me were asked by a young woman in the rear of
the crowd. Afterward she came forward and told me

something about herself. She was a Jewess, and a Socialist; she came from a sweatshop in Chicago to get a four years' training. She was going back to Chicago to her sweatshop people, an educated Socialist, to tell them that in Socialism and in Socialism alone was their salvation.

The literature of the Socialists far surpasses the literature of the Church. There are to-day fifty weekly and monthly Socialist papers published in this country, and one daily printed in Chicago. There is in one of our Western States a weekly which has a circulation of three hundred thousand copies, and upon occasion they will get out three million copies. Besides these periodicals, they get out tons upon tons of other literature. Nearly all of it appeals to the common man, the workingman, because it is written in the language of the people. Some time ago I spoke to a Socialist leader in one of our Western cities—a city with a population of three hundred thousand, where at the last election they nearly elected a Socialist mayor. They did elect twelve Socialist aldermen. I said to him, "How is it that you Socialists are so successful?" He replied: "We put nine-tenths of our campaign funds into literature. We have three hundred men, Socialists, each of whom has become responsible for a particular section of the city. They are pledged to get up every Sunday morning at five o'clock, summer and winter, for the purpose of making the rounds of their sections with literature printed in different

languages, which is inserted in the newspapers found
upon the front porches." Imagine, if you can, in
Chicago or New York, in Detroit, Philadelphia, or
in any other American city, three hundred Christian
men pledged to get up every Sunday morning at
five o'clock to go the rounds of particular districts
for the purpose of putting Christian literature into
the Sunday morning newspaper or under the door-
step of the working-people in their community, because they felt that the message of Christianity was
far more important than the message of Socialism.
I can not conceive of them doing it; can you? I
confess that I am not doing it. I am not asking
you to do it. I am telling you how it is that the
Socialists of the world are making the progress that
they are making to-day. They have training-schools
in several cities of our country, from which they are
sending out finished propagandists; men and women
who have been trained in every phase of Socialism—
Socialism in art, Socialism in literature, Socialism
in history. They talk with authority. They can
give a reason for the hope that is within them. And
when you tell the common people that Socialism is
an awful thing, you must be prepared to tell them
why it is an awful thing.

In some of our Western cities they have regular
preaching services on Sunday. They have district
Sunday-schools. They have open-air meetings. Last
year my friend, Dr. Ely, who had charge of the open-
air meetings of the Churches of Greater New York,

sent me a list of the open-air meetings to be conducted by these Churches during a particular week. I happened to have on my desk a copy of the *Worker,* the Socialist paper of New York City, which contained a list of the Socialist open-air meetings to be held during the same week. I ran a pencil mark around this list of meetings and sent the paper to Ely. For every open-air meeting conducted by the Churches these Socialists were to conduct fifteen, and yet these nearly one thousand Protestant Churches thought they were doing a magnificent work in bringing the Gospel of Jesus Christ to the masses of the people who were hearing about Socialism.

I am not a Socialist. It does not appeal to me, either as an economic or as a social system. Nevertheless there are some things about this question which it seems to me we must frankly face and confess. What should be the attitude of the Church toward Socialism? First of all, we must recognize the fact that a man has a perfect right to be a Socialist if he so desires. If he is convinced that Socialism is morally and economically sound, he has a perfect right to be a Socialist in this country. In the second place, we must recognize that it is quite possible for a man to be a Socialist and a Christian, too. I have no sympathy with the statement that a Socialist can not be a Christian. He can, and there are many of them. Furthermore, we must show the workingmen of this country that the Church of Jesus Christ does not stand for the present social system.

It does not uphold it. It stands for only so much
of it as is in accordance with the principles laid
down by Jesus. We have not quite reached that
ideal. Again, we must show workingmen that the
Church does not offer them the Gospel of Jesus as
a mere sop, or because we are afraid that some day
they may bring on a revolution. We must show
them that we are offering them the same Gospel,
with all of its privileges and obligations, that we are
offering to their employers.

These, then, are some of the elements which confront us and which challenge the Church of the
twentieth century. To make you understand more
fully our position in this matter, I desire to call
your attention briefly to four important facts.

First, the Church is slowly but surely losing
ground in the great centers of population. Nearly
every city in America is witnessing the removal of
its Churches from the densely populated sections,
where the Church is most needed, and this in the
face of the greatest opportunity that has ever come
to the Church in the history of home missions.
Within recent years, forty Protestant Churches
moved out of the district below Twentieth Street
in New York City, while three hundred thousand
people moved in, and they were all working-people.
I know it is said sometimes that the people in the
lower end of New York are all foreigners. I lived
there too long to be fooled by that statement. But
suppose it is true. Suppose they are all foreigners

—these three hundred thousand, besides the hundreds
of thousands who were there before they came.   I
heard of a Church that sold its property because there
were too many foreigners in the neighborhood; then
they sent the money to the Board of Foreign Mis-
-sions. If I were not on this job—to use the workingman's expression—I would become a foreign missionary. I believe in foreign missions. My wife
is a volunteer to the foreign field.   She is ready
to go.   But it seems to me that since God, in His
providence, has sent the foreigner to our very door,
He has given us the mission of evangelizing him;
and it will be only as the Church is willing to lose
her life that she will find it again among the masses
of the people. Now, if the tendency of the population is toward the cities, and if the cities are to
dominate the nation, and there is absolutely no question about it, it does not require a prophet or the
son of a prophet to foretell the inevitable result, if
this failure of the Church in meeting the city problem continues.

Second, underlying the spirit of social unrest
throughout the world to-day there is a deeply religious spirit among the masses of the people. In the
city of Brussels the Socialists have erected a people's
palace. In one of the halls just back of the platform,
and behind a screen, there is frescoed upon the wall
the form of Jesus Christ, with hand uplifted. It
is a very significant thing that while these Socialists
despise the Church, they have the greatest respect

for its Founder. I speak on nearly every Sunday afternoon to a mass-meeting of workingmen in some American city. The audience rarely numbers less than a thousand; often there are two or three thousand. Once there were ten, and again fifteen thousand men. As I have talked to these hard-headed American artisans concerning the supremacy of Jesus Christ in their own lives, there has come applause from every part of the hall, indicating that down deep in the heart of the common people there is a profound respect for Jesus. These people are religious, even though that religion may not be expressed in an orthodox manner.

Third, God is not dependent upon the Church for the carrying out of His plans for the redemption of the world. I was very much struck with the third verse of the hymn that we sang:

> "Yet these are not the only walls
>   Wherein Thou mayest be sought,
> On homeliest work Thy blessing falls
>   In truth and patience wrought."

Thus far the Church has stood the test of time. Her ideals and methods have been so far above every other agency that she has surpassed them in the race for supremacy. But at no time in her history has the Church's claim to be the truest representative of God in the world been undisputed. Other religions and other institutions have insisted that they, too, must be recognized as having the spirit of Jesus

Christ. The pride of the Jew suffered a severe shock when he was told that the miserable Samaritan was just as greatly beloved by God as he was. It required a distinct revelation from heaven to convince even large-hearted Peter that "God is no respecter of persons, but he that feareth Him and worketh righteousness is accepted with Him." It required an Ecumenical Conference, as we are told about it in the fifteenth chapter of Acts, to show the early missionaries that the Gentiles need not be bound by certain forms and ceremonies which were practiced by the Christians who formed the Church as it then existed. Often has God been compelled to rebuke those who considered themselves the elect in the matter of representing Him in the world. Francis of Assisi, Savonarola, Luther, Wycliffe, and Knox, and a long line of other men, were compelled to withstand those whose opposition was based upon a narrow conception of the true significance and the comprehensiveness of the kingdom of God. It was when the old Church of England seemed to be getting away from the common people that God raised up a man out of that Church who organized, originally, not a Church, but a company of men and women who have since become a power in the world. And the only excuse for your existence as a Methodist Church is the fact that you went out among the common people to minister to them; not simply to minister to their spiritual needs, but to their social and their economic needs. You read the life of John Wesley, and you will find that he was deeply interested in the every-day life of the common people.

Furthermore, the Church is responsible for the spirit of social unrest which exists to-day. And she must finish the task which she has begun. Some one recently said that during the past twenty-five years social unrest has increased threefold. During the same period, he goes on to say, the Church has increased threefold. Therefore, he concludes, the message and method of the Church in the matter of keeping down the spirit of social unrest has been absolutely non-effective. I agree with this statement, only my viewpoint is just a bit different. In the first place, it does not necessarily follow that because there is to-day three times as much social unrest, therefore social conditions are three times as de-plorable. Rather is the opposite true. No one would think of saying that because of the present chaotic state of Russia the people in that country are in a worse condition than when the tyranny of its rulers was accepted without any manifestation of opposition on their part. Russia is farther along to-day than she was twenty-five years ago.

I would point out to you that there are no labor troubles in darkest Africa. Curiously enough, the very missionaries that you are sending there are go-ing to create labor troubles and develop social unrest. If they fail to do it, they shall be untrue to the mission and the commission of Jesus Christ. They will point out to these people their low ideals, the low physical conditions with which they are satisfied. Then they will point out those higher ideals which Jesus Christ has presented to us, and, as a natural consequence, the great mass of heathen will become dissatisfied, and then there will be created among them a healthy spirit of social unrest. Bands will begin to break as they have broken in the past, and the people will leap forth out of their bonds and claim those higher and better things that Christ intends they should have. That has been the history of the Church. The Church is responsible for the social unrest of this twentieth century. She has created it. That has been her business, and because this is true, instead of denouncing the Church for her inability to keep down the spirit of social unrest, let us give her credit for having done the job, and it is a mighty good one, too. Social unrest is one of the most hopeful signs of the times. Without it there can be no real progress.

But this spirit of social unrest requires intelligent and unselfish direction, and it is at this point that the Church must be true to herself. I am not at all bothered about the spirit of social unrest in this twentieth century. I am not afraid of it. But it is just at this point that the Church is going to be most severely tested. Having created dissatisfaction among the people, is the Church now to step aside and permit the unprincipled agitator of materialism to come in and usurp the place which naturally belongs to her, or shall the Church go forward

in the work which God has given her to do, bravely
finishing the task which she has so grandly begun?
That is the problem as it presents itself to us to-day.

What may the Church do in answer to this challenge? First of all, we need to study the problems
of the people sympathetically. When our young
men go to the theological seminary to study for the
ministry, they study about the social life of the
Canaanites, the Hittites, the Amorites, the Perizzites,
the Hivites, and the Jebusites. And when they become our ministers, they preach about these very interesting people that lived so long time ago, and we
listen to them with very great pleasure—that is, sometimes some of us do. But when a man studies into
the social life of the people that live in Buffalo, for
example, and preaches about it, some dear brother or
sister will remind him that he might better preach
the simple Gospel, whatever that really is. I have
never quite found out. To me the Gospel of Jesus
Christ is as broad as humanity, and as deep as human
experience. Any narrow, stingy conception of the
Gospel of Jesus Christ is an insult to Jesus Christ
and a slander upon Christianity.

Study sympathetically, then, the every-day problems of this great mass of people who are understood
by the Socialists, who are understood by the trades
unionists, who are understood by those anarchists
who are quite ready to lead them into grave and
serious errors, as you so often put it. They understand them, but do you?

In the second place, we must stay by the people and help them solve their problems. Ordinarily, when we take up city mission work, we will organize a mission on a side street, in a dark, dingy, dirty building, and put in charge of it a man to whom we will pay about six hundred dollars a year, and then expect him to solve problems that would stagger many a six-thousand-dollar man. Then we wonder why we are not getting at the great social problems in our cities. We are putting our poorest men in these strategic centers, and then desert them, letting them fight their own battles, and sometimes we permit them to kill themselves in their efforts to help the people whom they have come to understand.

To do this we need more of the social spirit. This means more than merely being sociable, if you please. Oyster suppers, strawberry festivals, ice-cream socials, and chicken pie are not going to do it. It requires something else. We must make the people the end of our endeavors. We must talk less about building up the Church and more about building up the people. We must remember that the Church is a force and not a field.

I wish sometimes that I could hit our system of judging of the success of a minister in a city mission field. The Presbyterian minister is supposed to report to the General Assembly the number of people received on profession of faith. That is the criterion of his success. Your Methodist preacher must report to the Conference or district superintendent the same thing. If he does not "make good" in that respect, we question whether Brother So-and-so is really doing a good work in the name of the Lord. This standard takes no account at all of the larger work that that man may be doing as he lives day by day by the side of these poor people, who look upon him as their only friend in that community. Through him their problems are being solved, and if it were not for his life and his work, day after day, week after week, year after year, their lives would be a veritable hell. Let us change the basis of our judgment in regard to the work of these men who are standing by the people and helping them.

A little while ago I was speaking to a mass-meeting of workingmen in one of our New England cities. It was a theater meeting. A minister was asked to pray. The minister prayed something like this: "O Lord, we pray Thee, keep the little children out of the machinery in the mills and factories!" When I got up to speak, I could not resist the temptation; I said that I, too, would pray that prayer. "O God, keep these little children out of the wheels; keep them from having their young, fresh, sweet lives crushed out. But, gentlemen," I said, "do n't let's put the whole thing up to the Lord. Let us put it up to the Legislature. Let us put it up to the owners of the mills and factories, and compel them to keep the little children out of the wheels."

3

This business of assuming a holy tone and offering
a pious prayer, and then stopping there, is not the
method of Jesus Christ. Let us stay by the people
and let us help them solve their problems.

Third, we must socialize our teaching and socially
convert our membership. There is many an honest
Church member who has been converted spiritually
but who has never caught the social vision. He has
never been converted socially. There is a great difference between the two. There are many professing
Christians who believe they are keeping the first great
commandment, but who are altogether ignoring the
second, which Christ said was like unto the first.

We must supply competent leaders who will
direct the people in their struggle. We need a volunteer movement for home and city missions, as well
as for foreign missions. We need talented men and
women who have caught a vision, and who will say,
I shall consecrate my life to America, to the city,
to the solution of these great social problems. No
man or woman is too good for that kind of a job,
for it will require the best talent that God ever
gave anybody. O, that God might raise up such
leaders in our own beloved land who will help solve
the city problem, the labor problem, the immigration problem. There surely can be no greater obligation to strong men and women than that which
comes from our great country. Instead of making
a city mission field a stepping-stone for a so-called
better position, bright men and women should grasp

the opportunities that are to be found on every side of that apparently smaller field.

The Church must insist on Christ's method for changing social conditions. Jesus Christ lived in an age which was infinitely worse than this. Half the world lived in slavery. The philosophers of that period asserted that a purchased laborer was better than a hired one. Jesus denounced these conditions as no other man of His time dared denounce them. But instead of advocating another social system, He began to change the individual man. Josh Billings once said, "Before you can have an honest horse race, you must have an honest human race.". I think there is lots of horse sense in that expression. Before you can have an ideal social system you must have ideal men.

I need not say to you that I have the largest sympathy for the man who is living in an environment that is debasing and degrading. I would do all in my power to help him. But after everything else has been said, it is what a man is within and not what he is without that shall determine that man's destiny. No social system that would be satisfactory to our day and generation would be satisfactory to the next generation, because we are growing, and I praise God for it. Let me repeat it, Jesus Christ did not advocate another social system, but He laid down certain fundamental principles which are applicable to every generation, and these are the principles which the Church is to advocate, because in the end the social problem is a moral and religious problem. It will never be settled on any other basis.

Socialism and communism and anarchy are fundamentally moral problems. I would not attempt to give a definition of Socialism which would be satisfactory to every Socialist. But here is one that satisfies a good many: "From every man according to his ability; to every man according to his need." If that means anything, it means a life of service. Communism means the giving up of one's personal interest. That implies a life of self-sacrifice. Your anarchist believes that men will do right without having the strong arm of the law to compel them. Bomb throwing is not an essential part of anarchy. I speak, of course, of philosophical anarchy. That implies a high sense of love, of purity, of righteousness. Each of these presupposes a strong moral character, the elimination of selfishness, and the supremacy of love. Before any of them can ever be introduced there must, first of all, be a radical change in the selfish hearts of men. To change men's selfish hearts is the chief business of the Church, and because it is true, the Church has a most important part in the solution of the social problem. This is the principle on which Jesus Christ operated, and it is because Christ operated upon this principle that His power is coming more and more to be recognized.

Napoleon, exiled on St. Helena, turned to General Bertrand and said: "I know men. And I tell you that Jesus was not a mere man. Between Him and whomever else in all the world besides, there are no possible terms of comparison. Alexander, Cæsar, Charlemagne, and myself founded empires, but upon what did we rest the success of our genius? Upon force. Jesus Christ alone founded His empire upon love, and at this very hour there are millions of men who would die for Him." Jean Paul Richter once wrote: "The life of Christ concerns Him who, being the mightiest among the holy, the holiest among the mighty, lifted with His pierced hands empires off their hinges, turned the stream of centuries out of its channel, and still governs the ages."

Here is a company of men interested in the social problem, who are saying that if we are to solve it we must go back to Christ. Here is another company who say, "No, not back to Christ, but forward with Christ." But, whether it is backward or forward, it is Christ and Christ alone to whom we look for the solution of this social question. He is the court of last appeal. Who thinks of going to Socrates, or Plato, or any other philosopher of ancient or modern times, for the final word on the social problem? But if we can get a clear statement of Christ's concerning the matter, the question is settled for all time. Therefore we can afford to take our stand upon the principles of Jesus.

In this controversy, I can tell you who is going

to win. It will be that company of men who will accept the leadership of Christ.

Jesus has sent a challenge to workingmen. He is saying to them: "Follow Me. Accept My principles. Make them the controlling principles of your lives, and no power in all the universe can stop the onward march of the working-people of the world." He is also saying to employers: "Make My principles the ruling principles in your dealings with your employees and with one another. If you do, you are sure to win, because I am sure to win."

God grant that both workingmen and employers may come to Jesus Christ as brothers, and say to Him: "We, O our Elder Brother, accept You as our Leader. We will accept Your principles as the controlling principles of our lives!"

II

WOMAN'S CONSCIENCE AND SOCIAL AMELIORATION

JANE ADDAMS,

Director of Hull House, Chicago.

II.

WOMAN'S CONSCIENCE AND SOCIAL AMELIORATION.

WE have been accustomed for many generations to think of woman's place as being entirely within the walls of her own household, and it is indeed impossible to imagine the time when her duty there shall be ended or to forecast any social change which shall ever release her from that paramount obligation. There is no doubt, however, that many women to-day are failing properly to discharge their duties to their own families and households simply because they fail to see that as society grows more complicated it is necessary that woman shall extend her sense of responsibility to many things outside of her own home, if only in order to preserve the home in its entirety.

One could illustrate in many ways. A woman's simplest duty, one would say, is to keep her house clean and wholesome and to feed her children properly. Yet, if she lives in a tenement house, as so many of my neighbors do, she can not fulfill these simple obligations by her own efforts because she is utterly dependent upon the city administration for the conditions which render decent living possible.

41

Her basement will not be dry, her stairways will
not be fireproof, her house will not be provided with
sufficient windows to give her light and air, nor will
it be equipped with sanitary plumbing unless the
Public Works Department shall send inspectors who
constantly insist that these elementary decencies be
provided. These same women who now live in tenements, when they lived in the country, swept their
own dooryards and either fed the refuse of the table
to a flock of chickens or allowed it innocently to
decay in the open air and sunshine; now, however,
if the street is not cleaned by the city authorities,
no amount of private sweeping will keep the tenant
free from grime; if the garbage is not properly collected and destroyed, she may see her children sicken
and die of diseases from which she alone is power-
less to shield them, although her tenderness and devotion are unbounded; she can not even secure clean
milk for her children, she can not provide them with
fruit which is untainted, unless the milk has been
properly taken care of by the City Health Department, and the decayed fruit, which is so often placed
upon sale in the tenement districts, shall have been
promptly destroyed in the interest of public health.
In short, if woman would keep on with her old business of caring for her house and rearing her children,
she will have to have some conscience in regard to
public affairs lying quite outside of her immediate
household. The individual conscience and devotion
are no longer effective. In the tenement quarters

of Chicago, I am sorry to say that last spring we had a spreading contagion of scarlet fever just at the time that the school nurses had been discontinued, because it was supposed that they were no longer necessary. If the women who sent their children to these schools had been sufficiently public-spirited they would have insisted that the schools be supplied with nurses in order that their own children might be protected from contagion. So I could go on with a dozen other illustrations. Women are pushed outside of the home in order that they may preserve the home. If they would effectively continue their old avocations, they must take part in the movements looking toward social amelioration.

On the other hand, this contention may be equally well illustrated by women who take no part in public affairs in order that they may give themselves exclusively to their own families, sometimes going so far as to despise their neighbors and their ways, and even to take a certain pride in being separate from them. Our own neighborhood was at one time suffering from a typhoid epidemic. Although the Nineteenth Ward had but one thirty-sixth of the population of Chicago, it had one-sixth of all the deaths in the city occurring from typhoid. A careful investigation was made by which we were able to establish a very close connection between the typhoid and a mode of plumbing which made it most probable that the infection had been carried by flies. Among the people who had been exposed to the infection was a widow who had lived

in the ward for a number of years, in a comfortable
little house which she owned. Although the Italian
immigrants were closing in all around her, she was
not willing to sell her property and to move away
until she had finished the education of her children,
because she considered that her paramount duty. In
the meantime she held herself quite aloof from her
Italian neighbors and their affairs. Her two
daughters were sent to an Eastern college; one had
graduated, the other had still two years before she
took her degree, when they came home to the spotless
little house and to their self-sacrificing mother for
the summer's holiday. They both fell ill,—not because their own home was not clean, not because their
mother was not devoted, but because next door to
them and also in the rear were wretched tenements
and because the mother's utmost efforts could not keep
the infection out of her own house. One daughter
died, and one recovered, but was an invalid for two
years following. This is, perhaps, a fair illustration
of the futility of the individual conscience when
woman insists upon isolating her family from the
rest of the community and its interests. The result
is sure to be a pitiful failure.

In the process of socialization of their affairs,
women might have received many suggestions from
the changes in the organization of industry which
have been going on for the last century. Ever since
steam power has been applied to the processes of
spinning and weaving, woman's old traditional work

has been slowly but inevitably slipping out of the household into the factory. The clothing is not only spun and woven but largely sewed by machinery; the household linen, the preparation of grains, the butter and cheese have also passed into the factory, and, necessarily, a certain number of women have been obliged to follow their work there, although it is doubtful, in spite of the large number of factory girls, whether women now are doing as large a proportion of the world's work as they used to do. If we contemplate the many thousands of them who enter industry and who are working in factories and shops, we at once recognize the great necessity there is that older women should feel interested in the conditions of industry. According to the census reports, there are in the United States more than five million self-supporting women. Most of them are between the ages of sixteen and twenty-four, so that when we say working-women we really mean working-girls. It is the first time in history that such numbers of young girls have been permitted to walk unattended on city streets and to work under alien roofs. The very fact that these girls are not going to remain in industry permanently makes it more important that some one should see to it that they shall not be incapacitated for their future family life because they work for exhausting hours and under unsanitary conditions. One would imagine that as our grandmothers guarded the health and morals of the young women who spun and wove and sewed in their household, so the women of to-day would feel equally responsible for the young girls who are doing the same work under changed conditions. This would be true if women's sense of obligation had modified and enlarged as the social conditions changed, so that she might naturally and almost imperceptibly have inaugurated the movements for social amelioration in the line of factory legislation and shop sanitation. That she has not done so is doubtless due to the fact that her conscience is slow to recognize any obligation outside of her own family circle and because she was so absorbed in her own affairs that she failed to see what the conditions outside actually were. As one industry after another has slipped from the household; as the education of her children has been more and more transferred to the school, so that now children of four years old begin to go to the kindergarten, the woman has been left in a household of constantly narrowing interests.

Possibly the first step towards restoration is publicity as to industrial affairs, for we are all able to see only those things to which we bring the "informing mind." Perhaps you will permit me to illustrate from a group of home-keeping women who became interested in the problem of child labor. I was at one time a member of the Industrial Committee of the General Federation of Women's Clubs, which is, as you know, an association of women's clubs from all parts of the United States. We were very much interested in finding out how much child

labor prevailed in the various States in which no
legislation had been passed for the protection of children. We sent out questionnaires to all the women's
clubs, and among others we received a very interesting reply from a woman's club in Florida. We
had asked that the club members count all of the
children under fourteen who were at work in the
factories and mills in the club vicinities. The
Florida women sent back the reply that they had
found three thousand children in the sugar factories,
and they added that they were very sorry that we
had not asked them about child labor earlier, because
their Legislature would not convene for two years
and there would be no chance until then to secure
protective legislation. They evidently thought that
it was very remiss on the part of the committee that
they had not earlier called their attention to child
labor conditions. The whole incident is a good illustration of the point we would make. These women
had lived in the same place for years. The children
had doubtless gone to work back and forth right
under their windows, but they had never looked in
order to count them and did not even know they
were there. The Industrial Committee sent out a
questionnaire which said, in effect, "Please look out
of your windows and count the working-children."
The club women suddenly waked up and bestirred
themselves to protect the children they had thus discovered. Something of that sort goes on in every
community. We see those things to which our at-

tention has been drawn, we feel responsibility for those things which are brought to us as matters of responsibility. In what direction, then, should women at the present moment look towards a more effective amelioration for the many social ills which are all about us?

If they follow only the lines of their traditional activities, there are certainly three primary duties which we would all admit belong to even the most conservative women and which no one woman or group of women can adequately discharge, unless they join the more general movements looking toward social amelioration.

The first of these is a responsibility for the members of her own household, that they may be properly fed and clothed and surrounded by hygienic conditions.

The second is responsibility for the education of children, that they may be provided with good schools, or kept free from vicious influences on the streets, and as a natural result of this concern, that when they first go to work that they shall be protected from dangerous machinery and from exhausting hours.

The third is responsibility for the social standards of the community, implying some comprehension of the difficulties and perplexities of the newly arrived immigrant, and adequate provision for the cultivation of music and other art sources which the community may contain.

We have already touched upon the first line of obligation and the difficulty of securing pure food without the help of pure food laws on the part of State and federal authorities and the impossibility of keeping the tenement family in sanitary surroundings without the constant regulation on the part of city officials. If the public authorities are indifferent to wretched conditions, as they often are, the only effective way to secure their reform is by a concerted effort on the part of the women who are responsible for the households. Perhaps you will permit me to illustrate from the Hull House Woman's Club: One summer, fifteen years ago, we discovered the death rate in our ward for children under five years of age was far above the average, rating second highest of any ward in town. An investigation disclosed that, among other things, the refuse was not properly collected. The woman's club divided the ward into sections, and three times every week certain women went through each section in order to find out what could be done to make the territory clean. Of course it is not very pleasant to go up and down the alleys and get into trouble with people about garbage conditions; it takes a good deal of moral vigor and civic determination to do it effectively. Yet the members of the club did this day after day until they were able to gather sufficient material to dismiss three inspectors from office and finally to secure the appointment of a competent inspector. When the ward became cleaner, when the death rate

4

fell month by month, and each health bulletin was read in the Woman's Club, all the members listened with breathless interest. I shall never forget the day, three years later, when the club broke into applause because the death rate of our ward had fallen to the average. They felt that they had been responsible in securing this result, that the neighborhood had been brought into a reasonable condition through their initiative and concerted effort. Of course, the household of each woman profited by the result, but it could not have been secured through the unaided effort of any one household. One might use, by way of illustration, the impossibility of knowing the sanitary conditions under which clothing is produced, unless women join together into an association like the Consumers' League, which supports officers whose business it is to inform the members of the league as to garments which are made in sweatshops and to indicate by a label those which are produced under sanitary conditions. Country doctors testify as to the outbreak of scarlet fever in remote neighborhoods each autumn, after the children have begun to wear the winter cloaks and overcoats which have been sent from infected city sweatshops. That their mothers mend their stockings and guard them from "taking cold" is not a sufficient protection when the tailoring of the family is done in a distant city under conditions which the mother can not possibly control. Sweatshop legislation and the organization of consumers' leagues are the most obvious lines of amelioration of those glaring social evils which directly affect family life.

The duty of the mother towards schools which her children attend is so obvious that it is not necessary to dwell upon it, but even this simple obligation can not be effectively carried out without some form of social organization, as the mothers' school clubs and mothers' congresses testify. But women are also beginning to realize that children need attention outside of school hours; that much of the petty vice in cities is merely the love of pleasure gone wrong, the over-restrained boy or girl seeking improper recreation and excitement. In Chicago a map has recently been made demonstrating that juvenile crime is decreasing in the territory surrounding the finely equipped playgrounds and athletic fields which the South Park Board three years ago placed in thirteen small parks. We know in Chicago, from ten years' experience in a juvenile court, that many boys are arrested from sheer excess of animal spirits, because they do not know what to do with themselves after school. The most daring thing the leader of a gang of boys can do is to break into an empty house, steal the plumbing fixtures and sell them for money with which to treat the gang. Of course that sort of thing gets a boy into very serious trouble, and is almost sure to land him in the reform school. It is obvious that a little collective study of the needs of the boys, a sympathetic understanding of the conditions under which

they go astray, might save hundreds of them. Women
traditionally have had an opportunity to observe the
plays of children and the needs of growing boys, and
yet they have done singularly little in this vexed
problem of juvenile delinquency until they helped to
inaugurate the juvenile court movement a dozen years
ago; since then they have done valiant service, and
they are at last trying to minimize some of the
dangers of city life which boys and girls encounter;
they are beginning to see the relation between public
recreation and social morality. The women of Chicago are studying the effect of these recreational centers provided by the South Park Committee upon
the social life of the older people who use them.
One thing they have done is enormously to decrease
the patronage of the neighboring saloons. Before we
had these park houses, the saloon hall was hired for
weddings and christenings, or any sort of an event
which in the foreign mind is associated with general feasting, because the only places for hire were
the public halls attached to the saloons. As you
know, the saloon hall is rented free, with the understanding that a certain amount of money be paid
across the bar; that is, the rent must be made up in
other ways. The park hall, of course, is under no
such temptation and, therefore, drinking has almost
ceased at the parties held in the parks. If a man
must go two or three blocks to get an alcoholic drink,
and can step down-stairs to secure other refresh-
ments, it goes without saying that in most cases he

does the latter. The park halls close promptly at eleven o'clock. The city is, therefore, approaching the temperance problem from the point of view of substitution, which appears to some of us more reasonable than the solely restrictive method. Many of the larger movements towards social amelioration in which women are active have taken their rise from the interest the women felt in the affairs of the juvenile court, and yet this does not mean that collective effort minimizes individual concern. On the other hand, we often see a woman stirred to individual effort only after she has been brought into contact with the general movement. I recall a woman in the Hull House neighborhood who, although she had a large family of her own, took charge every evening of a boy whose mother scrubbed offices down-town every day from five o'clock in the afternoon until eleven at night. This kindly woman gave the boy his supper with her own children, saw that he got into no difficulty during the evening, and allowed him to sleep on the lounge in her sitting-room until his mother came by in the evening and took him home. After she had been doing this for about six months, I spoke to her about it one day and congratulated her on her success with the boy, who had formerly been a ward of the juvenile court. She replied that she had undertaken to help the boy because the juvenile court officer had spoken to her about him and had said that he thought she might be willing to help because he had observed her interest in juvenile court matters. Although the boy's mother was a neighbor of hers, she had not apparently seen her obligation to the lad until it had been brought home to her in this somewhat remote way. It is another illustration of our inability to see the duty "next to hand" until we have become alert through our knowledge of conditions in connection with the larger duties. We would all agree that social amelioration must come about through the efforts of many people who are moved thereto by the compunction and stirring of the individual conscience, but we are only beginning to understand that the individual conscience will respond to the special challenge and will heed the call largely in proportion as the individual is able to see the social conditions and intelligently to understand the larger need. Therefore, careful investigation and mutual discussion is perhaps the first step in securing the legal enactment and civic amelioration of obvious social ills.

The third line of effort which every community needs to have carried on if it would obtain a social life in any real sense, I may perhaps illustrate from experiments at Hull House, not because they have been especially successful, but because an attempt has there been made to develop the social resources of an immigrant community.

If an historian, one hundred years from now, should write the social history of America, he would probably say that one of the marked characteristics of our time was the arrival of immigrants at the rate of a million a year and the fact that the American people had little social connection with them. If the historian a hundred years hence used the same phrases which the psychologists now use—perhaps they will get over them by that time—he would say that our minds seem to be "inhibited" by certain mental concepts which apparently prevented us from forming social relations with immigrants. What are these mental concepts, this state of mind which keeps us apart from the immigrant populations? The difference in language, in religion, in history and tradition always makes social intercourse difficult, and yet every year people go to Europe for the very purpose of overcoming that difference and of seeing the life of other nations. They discover that people may differ in language and education and still possess similar interests. We would say that a person who went to Europe and returned without that point of view had made rather a failure of his trip. In the midst of American cities there are various colonies of immigrants who represent European life and conditions, and that we who stay at home know so little about them is only because we do not make the adequate effort. We have in the neighborhood of Hull House a colony of about five thousand Greeks, who once produced in the Hull House theater the classic play of "Ajax," written by Sophocles. The Greeks were very much surprised when the professors came from the various

universities in order to follow the play in the Greek
text from books which they brought with them. The
Greeks were surprised, because they did not know
there were so many people in Chicago who cared for
ancient Greece. The professors in turn were astonished to know that the modern Greeks were able to
give such a charming interpretation of Sophocles.
It was a mutual revelation on both sides. On one
side the Greeks felt more nearly a part of America,
and on the other side the professors felt that perhaps
the traditions had not been so wholly broken in
the case of Greece as they had been led to believe.
It would have been difficult for the Greeks to have
made for themselves all the preliminary arrangements
for this play; they needed some people to act as
ambassador, as it were, and yet they themselves possessed this tradition, the historic background, this
beauty of classic form, which our American cities so
sadly need and which they were able to supply.

We may illustrate from Italy, if you please, the
very word which charms us so completely when we
hear it on the other side of the Atlantic, and yet
it means so little to us in our own country. These
colonies of Italians might yield to our American life
something very valuable if their resources were intelligently studied and developed. They have all sorts
of artistic susceptibility, and even trained craftsman-
ship, which is never recovered for use here. I tell
the story sometimes of an Italian who was threatened
with arrest by his landlord because he had orna-

mented the doorpost of his tenement with a piece
of beautiful wood carving. The Italian was very
much astonished at this result of his attempt to make
his home more beautiful. He could not understand
why his landlord did not like it; he said that he
had carved a reredos in a church in Naples, which
Americans came to look at and which they thought
was very beautiful; the man was naturally bewil-
dered by the contrast between the appreciation of his
work in Naples and Chicago. And yet we need nothing more in America than that same tendency to
make beautiful the surroundings of our common life.
The man's skill was a very precious thing, and ought
to have been conserved and utilized in our American
life. The Italians in our neighborhood occasionally
agitate for the erection of a public wash-house. They
do not like to wash in their own tenements; they
have never seen a washing tub until they came to
America, and find it very difficult to use it in the
restricted space of their little kitchens and to hang
the clothes within the house to dry. They say that
in Italy washing clothes is a pleasant task. In the
villages the women all go to the stream together;
in the towns, to the public wash-house, and washing,
instead of being lonely and disagreeable, is made
pleasant by cheerful conversation. It is asking
a great deal of these women to change suddenly all
their habits of living, and their contention that the
tenement house kitchen is too small for laundry work
is well taken. If women in Chicago knew the needs of

the Italian colony and were conversant with their living in Italy, they, too, would agitate for the erection of public wash-houses for the use of Italian women. Anything that would bring cleanliness and fresh clothing into the Italian households would be a very sensible and hygienic measure. . It is, perhaps, asking a great deal that the members of the city council should understand this, but surely a comprehension of the needs of these women and efforts towards ameliorating their lot might be regarded as a matter of conscientious duty on the part of American women.

One constantly sees also, in the Italian colony, that sad break between the customs of the older people and their children, who, because they have learned English and certain American ways, come to be half ashamed of their parents. It does not make for good Americans that the children should thus cut themselves away from the European past. If the reverse could be brought about; if the children, by some understanding of the past, could assist their parents in making the transition to American habits and customs, it would be most valuable from both points of view. An Italian girl who has gone to the public school and has had lessons in cooking and the household arts, will help her mother much more and connect the entire family with American foods and household habits more easily, if she understands her mother's Italian experiences. That the mother has never baked bread in Italy—only mixed it in her own house, and then taken it out to the village oven—

makes it all the more necessary that her daughter should understand the complication of a cooking stove and introduce her to its mysteries. At the same time, the daughter and her American teacher could get something of the historic sense and background in the long line of woman's household work by knowing this primitive woman and learning from her some of the old recipes and methods which have been preserved among the simplest people because of their worth. Take the girl who learns to sew in the public school, whose Italian mother is able to spin with the old stick spindle, reaching back to the period of Homer and David; who knows how to weave and to make her own loom; such a girl's mother could bring a most valuable background into a schoolroom over-filled with machine-made products, often shoddy and meaningless. As the old crafts may be recovered from a foreign colony and used for the edification of our newer cities, so it is possible to recover something of the arts. We have in Hull House a music school in which some of the foreign-born children have been pupils for twelve years. These children often discover in the neighboring foreign colonies old folk songs which have never been reduced to writing. The music school reproduces these songs and invites the older people to hear them; their pleasure at such a concert is quite touching as they hear the familiar melodies connecting them with their earliest experiences, reminiscent perhaps of their parents and grandparents.

After all, what is the function of art but to preserve in permanent and beautiful form those emotions and solaces which cheer life, make it kindlier and more comprehensible, lift the mind of the worker from the harshness of his task, and, by connecting him with what has gone before, free him from a sense of isolation and hardship? Many American women of education are beginning to feel a sense of obligation for work of this sort. If women have been responsible in any sense for that gentler side of life which softens and blurs some of the conditions of life, then certainly they have a duty to perform in the large foreign colonies which make up so large a part of the American cities. I am sure illustrations occur to all of you as to what might be done in this third line of responsibility, for, whatever we think as to a woman's fitness to secure betterment through legal enactment, we must agree that responsibility for social standards has always been hers.

In closing, may I recapitulate that if woman would fulfill her traditional responsibility to her own children; if she would educate and protect from danger the children in the community, who now work in factories although they formerly worked in households; if she would in any sense meet the difficulties which modern immigration has brought us; then she must be concerned to push her conscience into the general movements for social amelioration.

III

SOME ETHICAL ASPECTS OF THE LABOR MOVEMENT

CHARLES PATRICK NEILL, PH. D.,
Commissioner of Labor of the United States.

III.

SOME ETHICAL ASPECTS OF THE LABOR MOVEMENT.

By the labor movement, as I am using the term in this discussion, is meant those collective efforts which wage-earners are making through the systematic organization of crafts or of industries' to secure control of the amount of wages they will receive, the hours they will work, and the conditions under which they will perform their labor.⁻

In a wider sense, the propaganda for Socialism is itself a phase of the labor movement; but for our present purposes, and merely for the sake of convenience, by the labor movement let us understand simply that movement which is embodied in the organization of wage-earners into trade unions or industrial unions.

This labor movement that we have just defined is now and has been for some time past looming very large on the social horizon. ' In one form or another its influence is being felt in almost every social relation.

Indeed, I suppose there are very, very few of us who have not had its existence—and probably its inconveniences, if not exasperations—brought home to us so directly that we have given it some energetic, and possibly heated, thought, and have probably formed some decided judgment concerning it.

But unfortunately, in far too many cases, the fact that one has passed conclusive judgment upon the labor movement does not at all imply that he has in the least understood it.

Because of the fact that the movement itself is aggressively militant, most of those without its pale have its existence brought to their attention most frequently through its concrete manifestations of an uglier or a more violent sort. They accordingly understand it in a narrow sense, and judge it from partial knowledge and in a somewhat angry frame of mind.

The various current views of the labor movement run quite a gamut. At one end of the scale we have the views of a large group of employers whose business has been very much interfered with and hampered by labor unions—and possibly in many cases very unfairly and unreasonably so—and who believe and proclaim that "trade unionism" spells ruin to our industries, destruction to our free institutions; that it is, in fact, treason of the most brazen and intolerable form.

At the other end of the scale we have the view of a school of sympathetic students represented by Professor Ely, who thus expresses himself:

"The labor movement, then, in its broadest terms,

is the effort of men to live the life of men. It is
the systematic, organized struggle of the masses to
attain primarily more leisure and larger economic
resources; but that is not by any means all, because
the end and purpose of it all is a richer existence for
the toilers, and that with respect to mind, soul, and
body. Half conscious though it may be, the labor
movement is a force pushing on towards the attain--
ment of the purpose of humanity; in other words,
the end of the true growth of mankind; namely, the
full and harmonious development in each individual
of all human faculties—the faculties of working, per-
ceiving, knowing, loving—the development, in short,
of whatever capabilities of good there may be in us.
And this development of human powers in the individual is not to be entirely for self, but it is to
be for the sake of their beneficent use in the service
of one's fellows in a Christian civilization. It is for
self and for others. It is the realization of the
ethical aim expressed in that command which contains the secret of all true progress, 'Thou shalt love
thy neighbor as thyself.' It is directed against oppression in every form, because oppression carries
with it the idea that persons or classes live not to
fulfill a destiny of their own, but primarily and
chiefly for the sake of the welfare of other persons
or classes. The true significance of the labor movement, on the contrary, lies in this: It is an attempt
to bring to pass the idea of human development
which has animated sages, prophets, and poets of all

5

ages; the idea that a time must come when warfare
of all kinds shall cease, and when a peaceful organization of society shall find a place within its
framework for the best growth of each personality,
and shall abolish all servitude in which one 'but
subserves another's gain.'

"The labor movement represents mankind as it
is represented by no other manifestation of the life
of the nations of the earth, because the vast majority
of the race are laborers." (Ely, pages 3 and 4.)

Fitting in somewhere between these opposing
views—precisely where I should not like to be called
upon to say—are some other views of the labor movement held by very considerable numbers. One recent essayist, a lawyer by profession, thus describes
the view that he has found quite common, and which
at least has the merit of simplicity:

"To the large public of the well-fed who live
by their wits and not by the direct application of
physical labor, the grumbling of the laborer against
the law seems delightfully simple. To this public
the whole grievance of labor, spelled with a capital,
is that the law forbids the heaving of bricks at
scabs."

Still another view, neither so depressing as the
one that sees only treason and menace in unionism,
nor so inspiring as the view of Professor Ely, but
a view comforting to its possessors and flattering to
their belief in their own judicial temperament and
sense of fairness, is represented in a considerable class

who express a very cordial, although very abstract, approval of labor unions, and believe that they believe in them, but who, as a matter of fact, disapprove in the concrete practically everything vital for which a labor union stands. An excellent illustration is thus given by John Graham Brooks, in "Social Unrest:"

"One of the grandees in the business world, who has publicly insisted upon 'the rights of labor to organize,' was asked in my hearing if he were favorable to trade unionism. 'Yes,' he said, 'I have always been its friend, but of course the union must be taught its proper place. It has nothing to do with the employer's business. If it dictates, it is out of its sphere. It ought to confine itself to mutual helpfulness, burial funds, and the like.' Of this kind of good-will to organized labor employers have abundance, yet it may conceal an absolute and settled aversion to every real object for which the trade union stands. This gentleman had an honest loathing for actual trade union when it gained strength enough to offer him the alternative of arbitration or of a strike. He had an imagined affection for a ladylike association which 'knew its place;' that is, which never questioned his own absolute dictatorship. He was fond of saying: 'There is no place for arbitration in my works, because I pay all that the business will afford. If they ask me to arbitrate, it is like taking me by the throat. With a highwayman there can be no arbitration.' "

To have any adequate comprehension of the real nature of the labor movement as it exists about us to-day, or any comprehension of the phenomena which accompany it, one must first get some appreciation of the spirit that lies behind it, the spirit that first gave it life and being and that still informs and vitalizes it.

For this understanding of the movement it is necessary that we once get a definite view of it against a certain historical background, without which it has no meaning.

Those without the movement rarely ever have any historical comprehension of it; but the leaders and the more intelligent of those within the movement usually have a very clear concept of its historical significance, and even the dumbest of the rank and file have an instinctive appreciation of the rôle that they are playing.

The most of us realize that this labor movement is a world-wide movement, but we do not realize that it is a world-old one. Yet this is the keynote to the whole subject, and until we do understand this, we can not correctly gauge any other aspect of it.

It is only the nineteenth and twentieth century phase of a struggle that is far more than twenty centuries old.

It is a struggle that has gone on persistently since the beginnings of the political history of society—a ceaseless and endless conflict—going back to the first efforts of the subjugated and disfranchised to overthrow oppression, to sweep away privilege, and coming down to the present struggle to secure complete equality of opportunity for all men alike to work out their highest individual destinies, and for each to live the deepest, the fullest, the richest life possible, and to develop to the fullest all the capacities with which his Creator may have endowed him.

It is a far cry from the early struggle of the human chattel to free himself from a degrading bondage which ranked him with the ox and the ass as a mere beast of burden down to a modern trade union conducting a strike for a higher wage or shorter hours per day.

But they are both scenes in the one continuous process of social evolution by which we have passed from the abject slavery of the earlier historical civilizations into the democracy of the Western world of to-day.

At each successive phase in that evolution the characters change, the stage setting looks new and strange; but the essential plot remains unchanged—the dominant motif remains the same.

To each age the struggle seems local and even sordid, but, viewed in the historical retrospect, it takes on that higher interest and nobler dignity that mark the sweep of the great forces which have endured through the centuries and carried humanity onward in its progression.

Let us now for a moment review certain aspects of that progress and note certain epoch-marking changes that have a special significance for our discussion.

Going back to the earliest stages of historical society, we find the institution of slavery, the foundation stone of the whole political and social structure of the ancient world. In this institution we have the fullest and most complete, as well as the frankest, recognition of the principle that has been fundamental in the social and political structure of the Western world for by far the greatest part of its history.

This principle was the accepted idea that certain "persons or classes live, not to fulfill a destiny of their own, but primarily and chiefly for the sake of the welfare of other persons or classes."

Slavery as an institution, let me repeat, represents the fullest and frankest embodiment of this idea.

The other extreme in social institutions is represented in the ideal of democracy—a society in which no hereditary differences of rank or privilege are recognized, into which every man is born free, and in which there shall exist for every individual the fullest opportunity for self-development.

These two social states, slavery and democracy, stand for the Alpha and Omega of political progress.

The first represents the starting-point at which we find organized society at the dawn of authentic history. The other represents the ideal towards which society on the whole has been tending ever since, steadily, ceaselessly, resistlessly, with many twistings and turnings and with some backward ebbs, but in the larger view always forging nearer and nearer to the goal.

We are still far from the attainment of the true ideal of democracy, but we are nearer to it than we have ever been before.

The institution of serfdom which succeeded slavery represents in the concrete a very considerable advance in human freedom, but so far as concerns the theory that underlay alike the institution of slavery and serfdom, it represents no such corresponding advance.

The difference in social theory between the two is a difference in degree rather than in kind. In serfdom the human being was no longer a personal chattel to be bought and sold, and eventually the serf came to have, even against his lord, a claim to his land and his lodging so long as he rendered his customary duties.

But the serf was attached to the soil; he belonged to a given estate, and passed from master to master with each transfer of that estate, the same, as the soil itself or the fixtures upon it. The estate, upon the produce of which the lord relied for his support and his comfort, was useless without the labor of the serf. The serf must therefore remain and give his toil to whatsoever owner the land belonged, and in every way subordinate his own welfare to that of his lord.

And the same principle applied to the members

of his family. His daughter, for example, might not marry, or his son study for the Church, without the lord's consent; for these were valuable additions to the force which tilled and rendered fruitful the estate; and the working out of their own lives or the fulfilling of their own destinies were subordinate consideration to the comfort and well-being of the lord.

This was, of course, merely the continued recognition of the same principle that underlay the earlier and grosser forms of slavery.

The next advance from serfdom towards freedom, like the one from slavery to serfdom, represents a concrete change in both economic and political status which is not accompanied by an equal change in the current social philosophy.

Thus, when the Black Death swept over England in the middle of the fourteenth century and carried off probably one-half of the working population, a situation at once arose that caused the current social philosophy of that age promptly to reflect itself in legislation.

By that date there had been a considerable advance towards actual freedom, and a class of wage-earners had arisen distinct from the serfs. In the great scarcity of labor resulting from the plague, the lords of the manors began to bid against one another for hired hands to till their estates, and wages began rapidly to rise. A golden era seemed about to dawn upon the wage-earning class.

But higher wages meant a greater share in the

wealth of the soil and a correspondingly less share
for the lord of the estate. The prosperity of the
wage-earner would thus have been at the expense of
the comfort of his lord and was, therefore, not to
be permitted. Such a change in the existing order,
such a readjustment of the social scale were not to
be thought of in the philosophy of the ruling classes
of the fourteenth century.

Straightway drastic laws were passed to force
the wage-earners back to their former economic status.
These statutes regulating wages and attempting
rigidly to fix the economic status of laborers were
enacted first in 1350, and re-enacted and re-enacted
with increasing severity in the determined effort to
force the wage-earner back into what was practically
the status of serfdom from which he had emerged.

These statutes fixed wages at what they were
before the plague had swept over England.

Laborers going from one county to another to
seek higher wages than could be secured in their
own neighborhood were sent to jail.

Laborers away from their customary place of employment without a written testimonal explaining
the reason for such absence and fixing the time of
their return to their regular employment were put
in the stocks until they gave surety for their return
to their employer.

Laborers leaving the service of one employer without his consent to take employment under another
for a higher wage were outlawed and imprisoned,

and might even be branded on the forehead in the discretion of the justice of the peace.

Here was almost as frank a recogniton of the right of one class to prosper at the expense of the other as was reflected in the slavery of a thousand years earlier.

It is true it did not recognize the property right in the person of another, as slavery had done; it did not recognize the sole and permanent property right of one individual in another man's labor, and the right to sell or transfer that other's labor at will; but it did recognize the right of one group, as a group, to the labor of another group upon fixed and definite terms and conditions, which terms and conditions were determined solely by the needs and wishes of the employing group.

It is the persistent recognition of the old idea of the right of one class of men to live their lives at the expense of another class and completely subordinate the destinies of that class to their own.

In the middle part of the sixteenth century the older principle seems to be passing away. The poverty of the working class had become so dire as to touch the heart of the Elizabethan legislator, and the celebrated statute of 1563 was passed apparently for the welfare of the wage-earner.

The statute is noteworthy, for it apparently marks a turning point in English labor legislation. All previous statutes dealing with laborers had been frankly and brutally in the interest of the landed

employer, but the preamble of this statute "shows
a tender concern for the welfare of the laborer, and
expresses a fear that his wages may occasionally be
too low."

By this statute the wages of labor were left to
be fixed by the justices of the peace in quarter ses-
sions, and both the employers and employed were
bound under heavy penalties to abide by the rates
of wages thus fixed.

But since in actual practice the fixing of wages
was thus turned over to what was practically the
employing class, the interest in the "hired laborer"
was more nominal than real. If he were not satisfied with what the solicitude of the justice of the
peace—usually a landed proprietor—might fix for
him as a legal wage, and he should enter into an
agreement with any of his fellows to secure a higher
wage, he exposed himself to the penalty of the pillory
and the loss of an ear.

This legal prohibition against combinations of
workingmen, first enacted in the fourteenth century,
remained on the statute books of England for five
centuries, and as late as 1800, a comprehensive act
was passed penalizing any combination or association
of workmen for the purpose of obtaining an increase
in their wages or a lessening of their hours of work.

It was not until 1824 that these conspiracy laws
disappeared from the statute books. So long as they
remained there, it can be said that the law continued
to recognize the right of one class to prosper at the

expense of another and made of the laborer the pack-horse of industry.

So near, indeed, does this come to our own times that there are many men still living who were born before these laws disappeared from the statute books.

So long as the economic condition of the laborer was one fixed by statute, so long as his oppression was founded in the law itself, the economic struggle remains merged and lost in the larger political struggle for personal freedom and equality before the law, and the course of history seems to mark a political rather than an economic progress.

It is only when political freedom has been gained that the real economic aspect of the struggle becomes clearly uncovered and focuses attention. It no longer appears as an effort to overthrow existing political institutions or to secure a larger measure of political or civil rights. The whole matter, then, stands forth clearly confessed as a class struggle over the distribution of the wealth that is being created. The disguise of centuries has been thrown off, and the real character appears.

The question of the distribution of wealth among the various social groups which co-operate in its production is not only the very root of our social problem of to-day—the basis for the social unrest and the social struggle going on around us—but at bottom it has been the great factor in social discontent since the beginning, and the moving cause in the social struggle that has gone on through the ages.

Economic spoliation and not political disfranchisement has been the real evil against which the masses have always been struggling. The political disfranchisement has been merely the means to accomplish the other object.

Thus, whether it be by the institution of slavery or of serfdom, or the later forms of legal regulation of the laborer, the real result was to enable his overlord to appropriate as large a part as possible of the product of the laborer's toil.

It was because this whole matter of distribution was regulated by law until practically the early part of the nineteenth century that every protest against the then existing basis of distribution—every effort to change it—had to express itself as an attempt to reform or overturn an existing legal status.

The real underlying economic struggle could thus only express itself in terms of political agitation or political revolt.

The nations of the Western world, as a matter of fact, have even now reached very different stages in this social evolution; in some the toilers are still fighting the preliminary battle; that is, the political battle. In others that battle has been won, and we are now in the thick of the economic battle.

One reason why the industrial conflict going on about us is both acute and bitter—with the probabilities of becoming more so—is because it represents a conflict between opposing ethical conceptions, between mutually exclusive theories of rights. So short has been the period since our social philosophy held and our statute books reflected the view of the ruling class that the laborer had no right to better himself at their expense, so recently has it been believed that concerted effort on the part of wage-earners to secure a larger share in the wealth of society was a conspiracy against the public good, that many of us have not yet adapted ourselves to the newer view.

Perhaps this is best seen in the field of domestic service. Recently in a certain neighborhood an organization was formed of women engaged in domestic service, and an agreement was made among them not to work over twelve hours a day. I heard a very earnest and somewhat excited discussion of the subject by a group of their employers, in which the action of the "servants" was denounced as "absurd," "unheard-of," "impertinent," "outrageous," etc.

When it was suggested to the employers that this was merely an effort on the part of certain fellow human beings to lessen their hours of service and obtain what they believed to be entirely within their rights, the reply was made that it was absurd to expect that the necessary daily work of a family could be compressed within the limits of twelve hours. It was then suggested that it did not necessarily follow that the work of the household was to be done within twelve hours, but that there were two other alternatives: either that more than one "servant" be employed, or that in families which could not afford the employment of more than one, the work in excess of twelve hours might be done by members of the family. This suggestion was indignantly repudiated and likewise described as "absurd" and "outrageous," and one irate dame asked if it was to be seriously proposed either that her comfort and that of her family should be sacrificed to the impertinent demands of a "servant," or that she or her daughters were to do any of the work of a "servant!"

Now, let us analyze this attitude of mind for a moment, for I think it fair to say it is wholly typical of the mental attitude of a very large proportion of those who are to-day employing domestic help. It simply means this, that those who are unable to employ more than one household worker feel that that unfortunate worker should sacrifice the greater part of her waking time to the comfort of that family and should be satisfied to accept this status as her proper and permanent rôle.

All this is only a more striking manifestation of the spirit represented by that believer in unions already quoted who insisted that they must keep in their place and must not attempt in any way to control the employer's business or interfere with his rights. But here is the very *crux* of the whole conflict. The employer's ideas of his rights and his employee's ideas as to these same rights are directly opposed to one another.

The employer insists that his business is his own, and that he will brook no interference on the part of his employees with his idea of what is best in the management of that business.

The employee holds that the wages he shall receive, the hours he shall work, and the conditions under which he shall carry on that work involve for him the whole question, not only of the material comforts of life, but of health and of leisure for self-development and for opportunities that he can offer to his children.

In a word, most that life holds dear for the wage-earner is bound up in the very things that the employer insists must be left to his untrammeled management and control. The wage-earner is unalterably determined, therefore, that he shall have some say—and a great deal of say—as to how the employer shall manage that part of his business which so vitally concerns the wage-earner's comfort, prosperity, and happiness.

We may well ask ourselves whether the vast, complex, delicate, and sensitive mechanism of modern industry and commerce can be made to work with any effectiveness if there be constant interference, and unless the management is left free and untrammeled in its control over the entire machinery. "Impossible," is the answer of most of those now in control of industry. But this is the old, old answer to every demand for the slightest change in our social structure. Thus, Aristotle could conceive of no other possible successful form of society than one based upon slavery. In the same way the mediæval ruling classes probably believed firmly and sincerely that a form of society more advanced than their own was a dream of a visionary. Similarly, volumes could be filled with impassioned, forceful, and even conclusive argument that a democracy based upon anything like universal suffrage was an impossibility. But Time, grim and cynical, has silently refuted the logicians from Aristotle onward. Slavery has vanished, serfdom is a memory, and a democratic society based upon practically universal suffrage *is* here.

It may be argued that after all democracy is working badly. It requires no unusual intelligence to see or to point out its weaknesses or its failures, and yet it is equally true that it is working far better on the whole than any social system the world has ever known before.

In brief, progress merely represents the overcoming of the impossible. In politics as in physics the impossible of one age becomes *un fait accompli* of the succeeding age and soon loses even its novelty and becomes accepted as quite the ordinary thing.

It may be argued that business can not be run as easily as government is run; that industry could not long tolerate such poor direction and manage- ment as we daily see in government. Those who hold this view may even be able to point out cases of interference with business on the part of wage-earners which has been arbitrary, unreasonable, and destructive, not only to a single business enterprise,

6

but even to a whole industry in a given locality. All this could be admitted, and yet it would be of slight consequence in the larger view of the argument.

Through the process of organization of wage-earners and collective bargaining, a school of training is created that in the long run will fit the wage-earner for his part in the newer system and bring to the front the most competent leadership, just as the actual experiment of democracy develops the traits that are necessary for its success.

It is frequently said that if all unions were like this or that particular one, or if all labor leaders were of the type of this or that particular leader, much more might be done in the way of joint contracts and of giving the wage-earner a larger say in the conditions under which he will work. I have heard organizations and individuals thus spoken of with approval which at an earlier period, and, in some instances, even within my own recollection, were regarded as radical and dangerous. I recall one particular labor leader, now dead, who, by those who knew him only in his later years, was regarded as a model of what a labor leader should be. In his earlier career this same man was the type described as a fire-brand. In the labor world, as everywhere else, the rule holds good that responsibility sobers men, that reverses chasten them, and that experience educates them. As a rule, the most conservative unions are the older unions, and although in many instances the newer leaders may seem to be abler than some of the older ones, it is only because they have begun with the heritage of experience garnered through the efforts and struggles of their predecessors.

But the strongest reason why a system of industry in which the wage-earner shall have more say in that part of the management which affects his wages, hours, and conditions of work is not impossible of attainment, is that such a system has got to be attained.

The age-long struggle for the lightening of the burden of the toilers, for a larger share in the wealth of society, and for a higher and better standard of living is not going to cease, and a system must be devised which will come nearer to meeting the demands of the laboring masses than the existing one.

The problem is a large one, and steadily grows larger and more acute, but we must either develop a satisfactory process by which, through some form of trade unionism and collective bargaining, the burdens of industry shall be lightened and the wealth constantly created by the joint toil of brain and arm shall be more widely distributed amongst those who co-operate in its production, or we shall find ourselves face to face with the menace of Socialism in one form or another. We may scoff at the fear of Socialism and assert that it can not thrive in America. Socialism has not thrived here as yet as in other countries, but this constitutes no guarantee that its history here will not be a repetition of its history in the countries of the older world.

There are numerous causes why Socialism has not made greater headway in the United States than it has, but one of the chief elements in retarding its growth here has been the success which the trade union movement has achieved.

The professed object of Socialism is to ameliorate the condition of the wage-earner, and the strength of its appeal for support lies in its power to point out in the concrete conditions of industry which press with crushing weight upon those who toil with their hands. In the same way, the strength of the appeal that the organized labor movement makes to the worker lies in the concrete successes that it has achieved in remedying his conditions. In many trades short hours, high wages, and good working conditions have been secured by complete organization, and the daily evidence of this success serves to stimulate the other less fortunate crafts to organize and to keep alive the hope that they in time will achieve a large share of that same success. The trade union movement represents the belief that far better conditions are entirely possible under the existing order, while Socialism represents the despair of any struggle made to better the lot of the wage-earner under the existing system and demands the complete overthrow of that system and its replacement by an entirely new social structure.

Let the trade union movement cease to expand,

let its success in having a voice in the management
of industry through collective bargaining grow less
and less, let its power to better the conditions of the
wage-earner appear to have reached its limit or to
be on the wane; in a word, let trade unionism confess its inability to continue to bring the hosts of
labor nearer and nearer to the goal for which they
have been struggling through the long centuries, and
the propaganda for Socialism will gain an impetus
which will transform it into a real peril.

IV

INDUSTRY AND RELIGION : THEIR COMMON GROUND AND IN-TERDEPENDENCE

GRAHAM TAYLOR,

Professor of Social Economics, Chicago Theological Seminary ; Director of the Chicago School of Civics
and Philanthropy.

IV

INDUSTRY AND RELIGION: THEIR COMMON GROUND AND INTERDEPENDENCE

INDUSTRY and religion, with education, state and solve the problem of human life when on common ground. Apart, much more in antagonism, they prove existence to be a tragedy. For what is industry? In human terms, it is the base-line, the rootage, the very condition of existence. And religion, with education, is the sky-line, the atmosphere, the horizon of life, which makes it more than meat and the body more than raiment, and without which life is not worth the living.

Now, apart from religion and education, and the human value with which they invest toil, its process, and its product, we have a body without a soul, lungs without any air to breathe, eyes without any light to see through, earth without atmosphere or sky. On the other hand, religion and education without industry give us only disembodied spirit, life on earth without the conditions of an earthly existence.

Throughout this discussion we have in mind the essentials of industry and religion, not their organi-

zations. We are considering their over-arching ideals
and their under-girding motives, which hold the con-
stituency of each together; not the Church or other
ecclesiastical expressions of organized religion, not
the organizations of either employing capital or employed labor. As such, then, have religion and industry anything in common? What have they to do
with each other? Is there any common ground
where they can, and ought, and must stand together,
if these two essential functions and ideals of human
life are to fulfill their part in the order of existence?

In the foreground of our discussion lies the portentous fact that the religions of the Western world
are entering the second industrial century of human
history. What that means we have scarcely begun
to imagine. But the first century of modern industry
stands in the clear. The nineteenth century was
ushered into the history by the whir of the power-
loom, which had then just fairly got to work. When
the hand-loom ceased to beat the measured tread of
all the centuries gone by, and the power-loom began
to set the pace of modern life, then mediævalism
ended and times altogether new began. So much
more rapid and radical than any other change
through which civilization has ever passed was the
transformation wrought by the introduction of machinery, the concentration of capital, the establish-
ment of the competitive order, and the subdivision
and organization of labor, that the appearance of

these new factors among men is recognized as "the industrial revolution." More than anything else which had yet been introduced into the world, they began to weave human life itself, not only into a new pattern, but into a new texture. In less than thirty years the new machinery virtually revolution-ized the world's life and began to change the very face of the earth.

We are far enough away from that abrupt break with the past to inquire whither we are being borne on the still rising tides of the new times. Whither away is modern industrialism bearing human life upon its resistless streams of tendency? From the course it took through its first hundred years, we can discern at least the direction of the channels through which its swift and tumultuous tendencies are forging their way into the times that are to be.

With the French Revolution the individual began to gain a new independence. That mighty revolt against the order of life which had for cen-turies merged the one man in the mass, forever broke up the ancient solidarity. Out of the death of feudalism came the birth of democracy. The demo-cratic individual was being born politically, when machinery appeared to give him a new world to conquer. All the inherent and attendant forces of machine-production conspired to intensify the inde-pendent individuality of those who exploited the tools of production. Even the many more who were left to work with their bare hands, without either the material or the machinery for producing their own living, were individualized as never before. The serf was no longer tied to the soil. Liberty of movement came in for the first time with the world market, and labor could go where there was the greatest demand for it. The individual became the new unit of society.

No sooner had the type of this new individual unit been fairly and firmly set than the same forces immediately began to put together those who had been separated from their groups. The industrial process of reintegration set in. The forces resident in or centered about machine-production and the subdivision of labor began to assert their superiority to the domination of the very individuals who created and until recently controlled them. The tendency of this new industrial society has been more and more from individual independence to the interdependence of man upon man, craft upon craft, class upon class, nation upon nation. Before the century was half over, industrial life swept away from unrestricted competition to a combination of capital and labor as inevitable and involuntary as the pull of the moon upon the tides. From the personal maintenance of the freedom of contract, the wage-workers were driven to the only possible exercise of that right by collective bargaining. Politically, the trend has been from local autonomy and State rights to national and international consolidation. Socially, whole racial populations have been blended more and more in huge cosmopolitan,. composite citizenships. The irresistible ground swell and tidal movement of the present quarter century has been away from individualism toward a new solidarity.

Yet beneath all the overlying turmoil and friction, injustice, and menace attending this rapid and radical readjustment, there is certainly developing a larger liberty at least for the class, a rising standard of living for the mass, a stronger defense against the aggression of one class upon another and a firmer basis and more authoritative power to make and maintain peaceful and permanent settlements of industrial differences. More slowly but surely there are developing legal forms and sanctions which not only make for justice and peace between employers and employees, but for the recognition of the rights and final authority of that third and greatest party to every industrial interest and issue—the public.

The Christian religion is inextricably identified with these human factors of the industrial problem. Its destiny is inevitably involved in these irresistible tendencies in our industrial democracy. Not for the first time is the power of the Christian ideal and faith being tested by its ability to solve the problems it has raised. For Christianity has ever intensified, if it did not create, the industrial crises which attended its birth and its rejuvenescence. The Christian evangel has all along held the ideal overhead and the dynamic within the heart which has inspired a divine discontent. Every now and then the Gospel strikes the earth under the feet of the common man, and he rises up and demands to be counted as one. Old John Wycliffe's categorical imperative, "Father He bade us all Him call, masters we have none," inspired "Piers Ploughman," the first great labor song; John Ball, whose field preaching was a declaration of rights; and Wat Tyler, who led the peasants' strike. Many another labor movement has inscribed no more nor less upon its banners than the Swabian peasants had upon theirs: a serf, kneeling at the cross, with the legend, "Nothing but God's justice." The progress of the democracy has often halted in passing the Church and listened at its oracles, to hear whether it could express Christian principles in terms of industrial relationship; whether it would let the worker be the man its free Gospel and its free school have taught him to know himself to be.

Protestant Christianity has from its very birth been persistently faced with the demand for the economic justice and industrial peace promised by the prophets and proclaimed by the Christ. By culminating in the correction of theological errors and ecclesiastical abuses, the Reformation of the sixteenth century must be admitted to have fallen short, however excusably, of the great moral and social results which would have been its legitimate consummation if its splendid beginnings could have been carried on and out. For it was made possible, more perhaps than by anything else, by the social discontent of the oppressed peasantry. Luther's protest found its most fertile soil in those suffering from the oppressive industrial conditions under which people had been robbed and beaten to the point of revolt. The economic side of the great Reformation is yet to be written. So far it has received due emphasis in the radical literature of writers avowedly inimical to Christianity.

At the rise of the evangelical movement in the eighteenth century, the Wesleys had no sooner raised that standard of reality in religion than they found themselves face to face with this same imperative industrial problem. The Methodist chapels and class-meeting trained both the leaders and the mass of the working people for their trade union movement, which was one of the incidental and most far-reaching results of the revival in England. The rise of the great middle classes to their activity in social reforms is due to this same evangel which brought the sunrise of a new day out of the leaden skies of eighteenth century England. Further, the rise of the factory system suddenly put the Christianity of the nineteenth century to the test of its supreme crisis. It was the evangel of the Seventh Earl of Shaftesbury, of Frederick Denison Maurice, and of Charles Kingsley, which, more than the Duke of Wellington's battalions, saved England from the revolution threatened by the Chartist movement to the evolution which has sanely and surely developed

the magnificent municipal and social progress of
Great Britain in the last quarter century.

The present crisis in industrial relationship tests
the capacity of the Christianity of the Churches to
adapt itself to the modern conditions of life and
marks the point at which it will either make another
great advance or suffer a sharp decline. It must
find terms of economic and industrial relationship
in which to express and impress its sanctions, if it
is to survive, much more guide and dominate life
in this industrial age. And our system and methods
of industry must find terms of religious spirit and
fellowship in which to justify their claim to be forces
making for righteousness and for the progress of
the race. This interdependence of religion and industry states the problem of finding common ground
on which they make each other possible and a religious industrial life actual in this age of the world.

There are at least three human interests upon
which both industry and religion set their value. At
these three points the industrial and religious valuation must either find a common denominator, or be
fatally exclusive of each other: In their valuation
of each single life, in their standard of living, in
the emphasis they lay upon union through sacrifice
as essential to progress.

Upon each human life religion has ever placed
a divine valuation. In both the Jewish and Christian faiths God identifies Himself with each single
self, by creating man in His own image and likeness,

and by standing in between each life and either self-
neglect or the aggression of others. When the king
of Israel was self-convicted of blood-guiltiness in
sending a common soldier to his death, he cried out,
as though he had struck at the very life of God,
"Against Thee, Thee only, have I sinned." The
Roman who was capable of coining the sentiment,
"Nothing that is common to man is foreign to me,"
was also capable of divorcing his wife because she
did not expose to death the girl baby born in his
absence, so disappointed was he that the child was
not a boy. Yet at that very time Christianity began
to invest every life with such a divine sanctity that
the law of every Christian nation has ever since
gotten in between the parent and the child not only,
but between even the mother and the unborn babe.
In America we put a valuation upon every child so
great that we can afford to make the school tax heavy ·
rather than to have any boy or girl grow up un-
educated. The right to life is so sacred that every
community in Christendom assumes the burden of
providing food, clothing, and shelter to every helpless
person, no matter how useless to self or others such
an one may be. More than by any speech, symbol,
or act of man, the cross of Christ sets God's estimate
upon the value of every man, woman, and child.
And it has imposed upon the religious conscience that·
sense of the worth of a life which is expressed in
what we call "the burden of the soul."

How, then, does the industrial valuation of the
7

same life accord with the religious value of the soul?
Our economists, indeed, estimate each able-bodied
workingman's life to be worth at least two thousand
dollars to the working wealth of the nation. But
in shameless inconsistency with these estimates of
our religious ideal and economic valuation stands the
industrial depreciation of the value of a human life.
Let the price-mark on a life be set by the overwork
of women, with which the courts are interfering to
protect the common welfare from the deterioration
of their offspring. Let the insatiable waste of child
labor be measured by the instinct of self-protection
which forces nations to protect themselves from the
industrial depletion of the very stock of the race.
Let the frightful industrial casualties in America
sound the depths of our own disregard of human
life and safety by the never published lists of the
dead and wounded, disabled and missing, which in
some industries exceed the casualties of the deadliest
battlefields of our worst wars. Let our conscience-
less heedlessness of the grievous burden imposed by
the bread-winner's death be arraigned by our re-
fusal to distribute that burden of supporting the
dependent families of the slain or disabled workers
as it is distributed in other lands between the owners
of the industry, the taxpayers of the State, and the
wage-earners.

Now, what makes work-a-day life a tragedy is
the hopelessly inconsistent disparagement between
the valuation which the industries and the religion

of the same people put upon the same life. The
claim of religious people to love the soul seems the
cruelest hypocrisy when identified with the heedless
carelessness for the very life of the same person. It
would seem that to make good its claims to bearing
the burden of souls, religion-must find concrete
measures of industrial protection in which to express its care for the lives of men. And yet until
very recently the working people of America have
been left alone by the influential constituencies of
the Churches to make their hard and heroic struggle
for self-protection. First in the field, hardest at
work has organized labor been to protect the religious and educational sanctity of each working
life, to regulate or suppress child labor, to shorten
the hours and improve the conditions of women's
work. But the efforts of others should not be forgotten. The splendid initiative of the Earl of
Shaftesbury in placing the factory acts on the statute
books of England two generations ago has led men
and women from all classes ever since, and never
more than now, to unite to protect and enhance the
value of life in such concerted movements as the
National Child Labor Committee, the Consumers'
League, the Visiting Nurses' Association, and volun-
tary agencies to co-operate with factory inspectors,
truant officers, and juvenile courts in the enforce-
ment of just and humane legislation. Thus the sanctions of religion and education upon the value of a
life are being translated in terms economic and in-

dustrial by every protected piece of machinery which keeps the fingers on the hand and the hand on the arm; by all the hygienic and sanitary conditions provided for in our shops; by all the efforts for industrial insurance; by all the life-saving appliances and conditions on the waterways and on the railways of the land, and wherever safety is in peril in the working world.

The standard of living affords another common ground on which religion and industry are found to be interdependent. In raising the standard of living to be compatible with the value of life, both industry and religion realize their ideal. By holding over every one's head the ideal of what a human life was meant and made to be, religion lifts the standard of that life, creates a divine discontent with anything less and lower, and stirs men to struggle singly and together to maintain and advance a rising scale of living which comes to be as dear as life itself. The response of industry to this ideal of religion is the demand for the opportunity to earn such a livelihood as will make the realization of that ideal possible. The struggle of working people to raise and maintain their standard of living is due to the best that is in them and not to the worst. "If this is the kind of a man or woman religion and education teach me to be," the worker naturally concludes, "I should be given the chance to earn the living of such a man or woman." Interpreted in human terms, "the standard of living" means the rest which the son of a working mother thinks she should have in her old age, the exemption which his wife should have from wage-earning in order to mother his children, the schooling his boy or girl should get before going out into the working world. The rising standards of living are due to the ideal which religion has taught us all to have of manhood and womanhood, fatherhood and motherhood, wifehood and childhood. Employing industries, which have too long and too widely united to hold down and retard the rise in labor's standard of living, have more and more to their credit unselfish efforts and achievements in lifting the standards of labor's livelihood and opening to ever increasing multitudes the opportunity and means of realizing it. Both among employers and employees the struggle to achieve the rising standard of living for the class and the mass should be sanctified by religion. It should be no small part of our personal and collective religious aim and effort both to protect our fellow-men from lowering the standard of their living and to help them raise it, and keep it rising, above a mere living wage, as far as the conditions of the trade or craft will allow. Until we thus translate our religious love of souls into our economic care for selves, religion will mean very little to those who are living in an industrial age.

A third common ground on which religion and industry are seen to be interdependent is defined by the fact that both have taught men to sacrifice in order to unite for the common good. Have we not been teaching, drilling, disciplining our men, women, and children, at home, at school, and at Church, by their loyalty to family, party, patriotism, and faith, to sacrifice self and stand together for the common good of all or any of them? Have we not invested with patriotic and even religious sanctity those who sacrifice themselves for "their own" folk, fatherland, or faith? How, then, do these virtues suddenly become vices, these heroes and heroines all at once become sordid conspirators when they combine, stake everything dear to each, risk all and stop short of the loss of nothing, in united action to save their own or their fellow workers' standard of living? They may do so in unwise or even unjust ways, but we submit that what is by common consent considered wholly meritorious in every other sphere for self-sacrifice can not be wholly reprehensible in that of industrial relationship, where it is hardest and costliest to exercise the virtues of altruism. What is attributed to the very best in men elsewhere can not be attributed to the very worst in men here. The "union" of laborers can not differ, *per se,* morally and as an economic necessity, from a combination of capitalists or the communion of members of the same religious faith. If at this age of the world, combination is necessary to success, where is the justice in forcing these competitors of ours to do their business with us as though they lived in that former age of the world when each

one could mind his own business without combining
with others?

It looks, then, as though the industrial world
has outgrown our moral sense, as though our ethics
are hopelessly belated. For we seem to want to
make our profits under the modern method of combining all available resources, while at the same
time insisting that our fellow workers shall deal
with us under the old, outworn, and discarded system
of individual industry. That is, we want others
to do unto us as we are not yet willing to do unto
them. It looks as though some of us were being
tried and found wanting. Of "times that try men's
souls" we speak as though they were to be dreaded
and yet belong to the "heroic age," but when we look
back upon them from some safe distance we are gen-
erally forced to confess that the "times" were not
more out of joint than that the "souls"—our own
or others'—needed to be tried.

These war times in industry are indeed to be
dreaded, but, like all great crises that turn the course
of history or personal experience, they too are heroic.
But the heroism should not be confined to the strikes
and lockouts of the irrepressible conflict. Industrial
peace should have its victories at the hand of religion, no less renowned than war. The cross and
its sacrifice, if they are to mean anything in this
industrial age, must be translated by religion into
terms of industrial conciliation, intercessorial medi-
ation, and sacrificial service, which will bring the

pact of Christ's own peace in human brotherhood out of fratricidal strife.

Industry has its cross as surely as religion. There is no way to the crown for either other than the passion of sacrificial service. Sacrifice, not only for self, but for others, is the only way by which either the strong or the weak can be crowned with that equality of opportunity which is the God-given right of manhood. Until industry takes up its cross with the self-sacrificing passion of religion, neither labor nor capital, employee nor employer, can really come to their own. Unless religion transforms its cross into terms of economic value and of industrial relationships, it can never hold its supremacy over human life in an industrial age. They must unite if either is to realize its ideal or function in human life. For they are interdependent, and only on the common ground of their community of human interests can they ever bring "the new heavens and the new earth" which God has promised to man through them.

V

CHRISTIANITY AND THE SOCIAL SITUATION

GEORGE PECK ECKMAN, D. D.,

Pastor of St. Paul's Methodist Episcopal Church, New York City.

V

CHRISTIANITY AND THE SOCIAL SITU-
ATION

LIKE every other vital organism, Christianity may be said to possess a kind of corporate self-consciousness, which includes, not only the conception of its fundamental and permanent mission, but also the conviction of its specific function in any particular and passing crisis. This feeling of the body may not always be identical with the opinions of certain individuals who belong to the organic whole. Just as the American nation has a view of its position and duty respecting the progress of civilization which is not shared by every citizen of the Republic, so Christianity in its corporate capacity may report itself as conscious of responsibilities and aspirations which do not receive the unqualified endorsement of all its adherents. Nevertheless, there is in every age of the world a dominant Christian sentiment which differentiates the Church of that period from the Church of any other period. This is Christianity's current feeling about its immediate obligation—its program for the day. The Christian commonwealth has moods, visions, expectations, and inspirations corresponding to the requirements of each successive stage in the progress of social evolution, much as men at different periods of their lives apprehend their personal relations to society according to the influences which are operative in childhood, youth, manhood, and maturity.

There was a time when Christianity regarded its first duty to be the refutation of the hostile criticism which was urged against its teachings. Right royally was that mission executed; and we are the beneficiaries of the results thus achieved. There is not a trace of philosophic paganism in the twentieth century, or a single fundamental position of materialism, which the early protagonists of Christianity did not meet and vanquish centuries before we were born; and it is only necessary to have recourse to the writings of the fathers to find weapons sufficient to annihilate every upstart enemy of the faith. But this is not the age of apologetics.

There was a time when Christianity felt its most imperative obligation to be the extermination of those heresies which had actually sprung from the marvelous fecundity of Christian doctrine; for the Bible is the greatest provocative of intellectual inquiry in the whole realm of literature. Nobly was this work of supplanting error with truth by the use of reason and revelation accomplished in the crisis which demanded it. But this is not the age of dogma-building.

There was a time when Christianity felt that

its immediate task was the consolidation and uni-
fication of its organic mechanism. On the model of
the Roman Empire it proceeded to erect a vast and
portentous institution, which extended its instru-
ments of control throughout the governments of
the civilized world. But this is not the age of ecclesiastical imperialism. The Roman conception of
the Church is an anachronism in the twentieth
century.

Other illustrations of the adaptation of the
Church to temporary conditions will occur to every
student of religious history, but we are now chiefly
concerned with the feeling of Christianity respecting the present age. The Church is not at this
moment so much interested in dogmas and heresies
and churchly machinery as with life in all its expressions, and specifically with community life in
its social and economic aspects. It is inspired by
that emotion which has been ascribed to its great
Founder, "the enthusiasm of humanity," a passion
which has broken out sporadically in all periods of
the Church's history, which manifested itself in the
philanthropic work of certain monastic orders in the
Middle Ages, and which has always characterized
the work of those valorous souls who have set themselves to redress the grievances of the depressed elements of society. But ours is pre-eminently the age
of humane effort for social redemption. The corporate consciousness of Christianity now reports itself as feeling a divine impulsion to antagonize and

eradicate every form of social evil, and the Church
undertakes this beneficent work in perfect harmony
with its central and permanent object, which is to
save the souls of men from the ravages of sin.   If
it be said that this ambition is simply a reflection
of the age itself—an effect of public sentiment re-
acting upon the Christian Church—it may be truth-
fully retorted that the humane spirit of the times
is the product of Christian teaching more than of
any other influence which has ever moved upon the
forces of civilization.

Very much has been said first and last about
the universal brotherhood of man.   Poets have sung
its blessedness and prophesied its recognition by the
world.   Demagogues have harangued about it in the
interests of their own political ambitions.   The
friends of liberty have embodied it in eloquent
periods.   Infidels and scoffers have dilated upon it
with unseemly enthusiasm, as though it were their
own special property; and all preachers of righteousness have longed for the actualization of the
prophet's vision and the poet's dream.   In our day
the idea of human brotherhood is more fully developed, and the prospect of convincing the world
that humanity is one is brighter than ever before.
But when we hear some social reformer, who ig-
nores Christianity, declaiming on this doctrine, as
though it were a discovery of the last decade, or
the re-discovery of principles hatched out in the
ferment of the French Revolution, we are false to

historic accuracy if we do not protest that to the
religion of Jesus Christ alone is the world indebted
for the plainest and the most persistent teaching of
the truth that all men are equal and kin. The characteristic Christian activity of our times is simply
a recrudescence of the original social teachings of
Jesus, and their application in a more intense and
practical fashion than has been possible in any
previous age of the Church. The current situation shows how opportune is this social awakening
of organized Christianity.

It is impossible to measure the ocean in a pint
cup, though its characteristics may be described in
a few paragraphs. It is equally futile within the
compass of this discussion to undertake a complete
portrayal of the present social crisis. Yet its salient
features may be roughly defined. Like the car-
toonist, we may give effects by broad outlines and
huddled masses of color. Here are multitudes of
starving, naked, vicious poor to be set over against
colossal individuals with wealth piled up beyond the
dreams of avarice. Here are grinding, maddening
sweatshops in one street, and the glittering equipages,
the spacious dwellings, and the circumstantial pomp
of the rich in another. Ten millions of exceedingly
poor people, living below the line of physical efficiency, fifty per cent of whom are just skirting the
edge of actual distress, the sociological experts tell
us, exist in the richest land in the world. Four
millions of persons in our country are wholly de-

pendent upon some form of public charity. More
than sixty thousand families on Manhattan Island
were evicted from their homes in a single year on
account of failure to pay their rent. One-tenth of
all who die each year in the same territory are buried
at public expense. Nine per cent of the families
of the United States own seventy-one per cent of
the wealth of the nation. Nearly two millions of
children under fifteen years of age are engaged in
manual labor unsuited to their tender ages. The
figures are most impressive. Here are capitalists
scowling at the laborer, and workingmen's unions
snarling and snapping at the money power. Here
are the gigantic aggregations of corporate enterprise
controlled by single minds, over against menacing
combinations of laboring men, the ranks in both these
lines being swayed by crude selfishness. Here are
the sins of refined criminals, who are manipulating
securities and ruining the unwary in what is known
as high finance, paralleled on the other side by the
dishonesty of the masses, who show little respect for
the rights of property. Between these conflicting
interests stands the Church, fretted and worried by
all, seeking to make peace and order for all, and
attaining, it must be confessed, only a partial success; for it must be admitted that at the moment
the Church has not a firm grasp on either extreme
of society; and one remembers the social designa-
tion made by Oliver Wendell Holmes of "the very
rich, who are apt to be irreligious; the very poor,

who are apt to be immoral." That the inordinately wealthy should not be very religious is not surprising. These are the persons who give color to Cardinal Manning's definition of society as "a conspiracy of fools, fashions, custom, mutual flattery, eating, drinking, and refined hardness of heart," and who also give support to the declaration of Ralph Waldo Emerson that, "Society is a conspiracy against the manhood of every one of its members." The Church could, perhaps, reconcile itself to the alienation of the very rich, when it recognizes the relative paucity of their numbers and the natural tendency of wealth to efface spiritual appetites; but the separation of manual workers from the Church is nothing short of appalling, for the Church can no more thrive without them than they can flourish without it.

It is useless to argue that such an alienation of wage-workers in vast numbers has actually occurred, since every careful student of our times is aware of it, and any observer may be convinced of it who will investigate the personnel of the average Christian congregation. Doubtless it is possible to find certain localities where industrial pursuits predominate, in which the Church does still exercise a very large influence over the working class technically considered; but the general attitude of workingmen, particularly those who in such great numbers are identified with the labor union, is confessedly unfriendly. In most of our great industrial

8

centers the bulk of the laboring people are not in fellowship with the Church. Exception, perhaps, ought to be made respecting Roman Catholic workingmen. The grasp of Rome upon childhood, which projects itself with almost unfailing strength into the mature life of those whom it has trained, holds multitudes of workingmen to at least a nominal adherence to the Church. Some of the more recent expressions of the Roman Catholic leaders on the social question have had a tendency to lessen this power, but Rome can be counted upon so to adjust her policy to current needs as ultimately to overcome the disintegrating influence of such a mistaken program. We are now speaking specifically of the attitude of those workingmen who might be supposed by birth and tradition to be within the reach of the Protestant Church.

We are familiar with the strictures which these men pass upon the Church. They declare that preachers, and congregations are held in complete bondage to the present industrial system, that the Church is under the domination of wealth or of the middle class; and that laborers, even if welcomed to divine service, have little influence in shaping the policy and managing the affairs of the Church. They say that the Churches are doing comparatively little to help them in their struggle against what they call the aggressions of capital, but, on the other hand, are catering to those capitalists who are trying to subsidize institutions of learning by bestowing fortunes upon them which they have wrung from the people by dishonest means, and are seeking to induce those colleges and universities to teach the rising generation a false system of economics and a cruel social regime. They confess that they have lost their belief in the authority of religion, because they contend that authority has been employed chiefly to quiet the masses and to make them content with their lot. They say that the Church is "the bulwark of the property-holding class, and the theologians are distracting the minds of the unfortunate by the promise of prosperity hereafter." They fancy that the Church has prostituted the Christian religion to the interests of the controlling class. According to one of their writers, "The cross, once a symbol of suffering, is now a symbol of slavery."

Growing bold in their sense of wrongs suffered, and in the consciousness of their own might, these men are now proposing to fight their battles alone. They remind one of the monk in Daudet's story, who, being attacked by a bandit, rolled up his sleeves and offered this prayer: "O Lord, all I ask of Thee is that Thou wilt remain neutral, and I will manage the rest." This strikes off the general attitude of organized labor toward the Church. Of course such a position is a tragic mistake. A recent writer on labor movements, who is himself in perfect sympathy with them, has stoutly declared that the chief want of labor unions to-day is religion. John Graham

Brooks has called attention to the fact that, in his fantastic dream called "Looking Backward," Edward Bellamy could find no other way to usher in his social order than by a kind of revival of religion. Kingsley and Maurice, in England, constantly declared that no permanent improvement of the workingman's condition could be accomplished until his own personal character had been elevated. No bettering of a man's environment can bring him enduring benefit without a corresponding moral exaltation from within. That this principle is true, the best sociologists universally concede. Now, the Church is unquestionably set to the task of effecting this moral and spiritual uplift; but if the connection between the Church, which is the custodian of religious teaching, and the masses, who are to be taught, is sundered, the situation is sufficiently serious to awaken the alarm of every thoughtful Christian.

Not only is the Church separated from an immense proportion of organized laborers; she is also in a large degree supplanted in the affections of these people by modern Socialism. We have not been long acquainted in any practical way with this cult in America, but its progress among us during the last few years has been very rapid. The number of Socialists in the world to-day is estimated at twenty-five millions, and records show that not less than eight millions of men have voted a Socialistic ticket, of whom more than half a million live in the United States. These figures do not measure the extent of Socialism's influence. Multitudes, who, bound by party ties which they venerate, do not support it at the polls, nevertheless cherish its principles in their hearts. When the present German emperor ascended his imperial throne, he said to Bismarck: "We will make short work of the Socialist-movement. Leave that to me; I shall win them over to my side inside a year." Nearly two decades have passed since then, and the Socialistic Party in Germany has more than doubled. It is estimated that fully one-quarter of the German people are affected by its ideals. The status of Socialism in Germany represents the general situation throughout Europe, though conditions are not so acute in all quarters. The contemporary situation in Russia speaks with tremendous emphasis. The Socialist propaganda has not flourished so luxuriantly in America, owing doubtless to our free institutions, but it has constantly progressed, and its influence is not to be measured by that vote of half a million. The whole brood of organized labor is more or less impregnated with its teachings. The sensational journals have fostered it, and these are the sheets which are read in the main by workingmen. The revolutionary sentiments expressed in these papers are cordially and perhaps unthinkingly endorsed by the great army of their readers. Thousands of working people who could not give a systematic account of theoretical Socialism are saturated with its sentiments.

But now a strange and portentous transformation has been occurring in Socialism itself. As is well known, its modern revival commenced on a practically atheistical platform. The philosophy of Karl Marx is bald materialism, and the oft-repeated sayings of the earlier school of Socialists sufficiently indicate their hostility to religion. But a great change has come over the tone of Socialists in this respect. They confess that they find religious convictions intrenched in the deeper nature of man, and that religion itself is much larger than the Church which teaches it. "It seems to be fundamental to the constitution of man. Possibly he is under a delusion, but he is wedded to his folly." It is a race characteristic and can not be ignored. Therefore, an attempt is now being made to employ religious forms in the service of Socialistic ideals, and Socialism itself is coming to assume the nature of a religion. As Francis Peabody says: "It is not enough to say that Socialism is indifferent to religion; it undertakes to provide a substitute for religion. It is a religion, so far as religion is represented by a philosophy of life to which men give themselves with passionate attachment. . . . It offers itself as an alternative to the Christian religion." In this fact lies its real danger at this hour. Once a defiant enemy, it has now taken on the very livery of religion. Dr. Thomas C. Hall says that "It is in Socialism that organized Christianity has its most serious and determined rival."

He bids us remember "that Socialism is not simply a political economy, nor yet even a philosophy of society, nor a scheme of reform. Socialism is a religious faith, and is being embodied in a religious organization." Its adherents are possessed of an immense enthusiasm. They are captivated by a sublime idealism such as inspired the primitive Christians. They are entranced with visions of a world redeemed from selfishness. They anticipate by faith the consequences of a readjustment of the social order on a new basis. Their orators speak with conviction and their congregations applaud with enthusiasm principles which any Christian pulpit might utter with honor to itself and profit to its audience. They sing lustily in praise of philanthropy. Socialism now has its hymn-books and its substitutional forms of worship. It spends thousands of dollars on literature for free distribution. Its adherents expect to win. They are as confident as Christians ever were. Socialism is an aggressive competitor of the Church, and its doctrines present such a close resemblance to those of Christianity as to make the competition very serious. A French writer has said, "If the people turn away from the Churches, it is because they possess in themselves the crude germs of a religion more grand than that which the Churches preach." It must be confessed that, if you remove the incubus of practical agnosticism from Socialism and strip off the barnacles of Utopian impossibilities which have clustered about it, the similarity between the saner teachings of the Socialist and the social program of Jesus of Nazareth will be remarkable.

It would, therefore, seem to be the strategic need of the hour to establish some bond of affiliation between the Christian Church, which is the natural custodian of Christ's social teachings, and the vast body of men who look to the Socialistic propaganda for their relief. The Christian teacher knows that what these complaining millions require is a personal alliance with Jesus Christ. The working class are looking for an advocate who shall possess three qualifications: First, he must be so thoroughly identified with them as a class as to be able to sympathize with them and understand their needs. Second, he must be powerful enough to put into operation forces which will ultimately remedy the evils under which they groan. Third, he must be wise enough to give them a philosophy of life which shall enable them to bear their burdens without fainting until relieved. Now, Jesus answers these demands with an exactitude which is nothing short of the marvelous. He was the son of a carpenter. It is fancied that He might have belonged to some artisan guild in Nazareth. He has dignified labor by Himself engaging in common toil. In His human career He came into perfect sympathy with mankind at every point. He enunciated principles which through the centuries since His earthly sojourn have operated in all civilized lands to mitigate the ills of the oppressed and to alleviate the condition of the toiling class.

The story of humane progress for nearly two thousand years is virtually a record of Christ acquiring the mastery of society. Illustrations of this are so numerous and so obvious that they require no citation here. Even Socialistic leaders themselves, though hostile to the Church, are ready to concede the influence of Jesus on the development of civilization. Finally, Jesus has given to the world a philosophy of human life which makes any kind of existence tolerable if lived apart from sin. He has said that "a man's life consisteth not in the abundance of the things which he possesseth." He has shown the incalculable value of every individual soul. The slave who cherishes His teachings may look up under the taskmaster's lash and remember that he is great with the greatness of God Himself. Knowing the workingman and his problems, sympathizing with him in his distresses, evidencing His power to assist him by what His scepter has already accomplished in the world, offering him a view of human life which wonderfully enhances the sense of self-respect, Jesus is the one supreme Protagonist of the labor class. The Socialist in his better moods will acknowledge this, while he still protests that the Church which Christ founded is alienated from the class to which He and His disciples belonged.

The peril of the workingman's estrangement from the Church is accentuated by the undoubted hostility of many capitalistic leaders toward organized labor. The wrongs under which the artisan smarts may be exaggerated in his thought by reason of his comparison of the little he obtains from his toil with the much which comes to the money-power as the result of his labor. Yet his sense of injury is sufficiently real. If it were not for the influence of religious sentiment, which exists to some degree in every man's breast, the enormous abyss which stretches between the condition of the very poor and the estate of the rich would so irritate the discontented masses as to drive them to frenzy and impel them to tear into fragments the fabric of our social order. Unless the Church can increase her restraint upon the selfishness of those who are in control of the sources of wealth, and harmonize the differences of the extremes of society by abating their cause, we may look for such a revolution as shall endanger the very life of our Republic.

To avert this peril it is imperative that a point of friendly contact should be established between organized Christianity and the millions who in the present crisis are severed from the Church chiefly through misunderstanding. This demand can be fully met by the fearless proclamation of the social teachings of Jesus and the scrupulous application of those doctrines to the problems which vex our social system.

One of the most mischievous errors which has crept into the Christian Church is the blunder of supposing that the religion of Christ consists wholly or even chiefly of belief in a set of doctrines, and the performance of public and private acts of worship. There is no need to underestimate the importance of creeds or of religious observances. If they are of slight value, it is difficult to see why an order of ministers should be created or money should be spent in the erection of churches. But it is mere fact to declare that a man could be perfectly orthodox in faith, and absolutely punctilious in religious observances, and still be as far from vital Christianity as a pagan who had never heard the name of Jesus or the title of the Christian Church. Indeed, it is even possible to conceive of a pagan who, living under certain conditions, and following certain moral and social ideals, would be a better Christian in the essentials of that term than a nominal adherent of Jesus, whose orthodoxy was bullet-proof, but whose social ideas were faulty. Dean Stanley writes: "It used to be said in the wars between the Moors and the Spaniards that a perfect character would be the man who had the virtues of the Mussulman and the creed of the Christian. But this is exactly reversing our Lord's doctrine. If the virtues of the Arab were greater than the virtues of the Spaniards, then, whether they accepted Christ in word or not, it was they who were the true believers, and it was the Christians who were the infidels." In a similar vein, and with equal truth, it may be maintained that Socialists whose teachings are in harmony with the philanthropic ideals of Jesus are Christians in effect, though they are schismatics from the Church, while conventional churchmen may be pagan in fact, though Christian in creed, if they are at variance with the precepts of Christian humanity. If these seem to be revolutionary statements, it will be well to examine Christ's own words.

William Henry Channing said that Jesus Christ did not understand His own religion. As a bald statement, indicating inferior intelligence in Jesus, this declaration must be repudiated. But it is easy to believe that Jesus would not be able to understand much of what passes current as His religion in our day. He would be puzzled to determine why it clings to His *name* since it has abandoned His *principles*. It is easy to discern some of the things which Jesus understood His religion to contain. One day Christ's disciples observed Him at prayer, and said to Him, "Lord teach us to pray;" and He did so in words the content of which has sometimes been forgotten. "After this manner, therefore, pray ye, Our Father which art in heaven, hallowed be Thy name," and so following. At the beginning, then, Jesus taught that God is our Father. Max Müller calls that doctrine the distinctive peculiarity of the Christian religion. It is a theological position which affects a great many things. It interprets everything else said about God in the Bible. If God is a great Sovereign, Judge, and Law-giver, it is His Fatherhood which determines what kind of King, Judge, and Lawgiver He is. When one prays,

"Thy kingdom come, Thy will be done," it is a paternal kingdom he desires to see triumphant. It is the will of a Father he longs to have executed. That prayer also interprets everything else the Bible says about man. If a man is a sinner, destitute of original righteousness, lost and undone, an alien and a rebel, we know what kind of alien and rebel he is. He is a lost child, a rebellious son, a wayward offspring. He is not a homeless orphan. God is his Father. That emphasizes man's inherent worth as much as it distinguishes God's loving kindness. The human stock has fearfully degenerated. But it is still marked with the features of a divine paternity.

When Rudyard Kipling was supposed to be dying in one of our New York hotels, he was heard to mutter something under his breath. His nurse drew near to his bedside and said, "Do you want anything?" "Yes, I do," he said; "I want my Heavenly Father; He alone can care for me now!" It was Jesus who taught him to say that, and He who has taught the whole world that any kind of humanity, in any part of the earth, living under any condition whatsoever, has as good a right as Rudyard Kipling to say, "I want my Heavenly Father."

Now, people who have the same father are customarily called brothers and sisters. It is possible to defy the laws of consanguinity and to deny the obligations of kinship. But Jesus perpetually protests against this folly, asserting at the outset of His teachings that God is humanity's Father, and that humanity is one in eternal brotherhood. It is a very grave question whether any man is justified in using the Lord's Prayer who will not admit this much.

One day a scribe came to Jesus and asked, "Which is the first commandment of all?" The Master replied, "Thou shalt love the Lord thy God with all thy heart, and with all thy soul, and with all thy mind, and with all thy strength. This is the first commandment; and the second is like unto it, namely, this, 'Thou shalt love thy neighbor as thyself. There is none other commandment greater than these.'" According to Jesus, the duties of religion are comprehended by these two precepts, of which it has been said that the first is theology and the second is sociology, but of which we may say that the whole is religion as Jesus understood it. It is noticeable that the only emphasis placed upon the first commandment is that it is *mentioned first,* while Jesus was always reiterating in one form or another the never-ending demand for love to men. If it be said that he who loves God supremely will inevitably love his fellow-man, it must be remembered that men have often professed to love God with all their hearts who have felt an obvious contempt for humanity; and that he who loves his neighbor as himself will undoubtedly love God with a pure and perfect devotion. Indeed, if one should take Christ's words

alone, he would be convinced that Jesus placed more
weight upon loving humanity than upon loving God.
He referred to the former far more often than to
the latter. The fact is, they are two hemispheres of
the same truth, and no attempt must be made to
divorce them.

That there might be no doubt concerning the
full extent of this commandment about the treatment
of one's neighbor, Jesus used an illustration to de-
fine the term "neighbor." He did this for the benefit
of a lawyer, and no lawyer has ever had a mind
tortuous enough to misunderstand it. It was the
story of the Good Samaritan, which every one ad-
mires, but which few pattern after. If a Turkish
bigot should nurse a wounded Armenian or Bulgarian
Christian, putting him in his own bed, and washing his wounds with his own hands, it would be
no more wonderful than that this Samaritan should
have cared for the injured Jew, and paid his hotel
bill. And Jesus said, in effect, "There's your model
of righteousness. Go, thou, and do likewise." And
the priest and the Levite who abandoned their own
countryman, though they were the very quintessence
of orthodoxy, it is implied, were the most unmiti-
gated heathen.

One day Jesus stood up in the synagogue at
Nazareth, where He had been brought up, and read,
"The Spirit of the Lord is upon Me, because He hath
anointed Me to preach the Gospel to the poor; He
hath sent Me to heal the broken-hearted, to preach

deliverance to the captives, and recovering of sight to the blind, to set at liberty them that are bruised, to preach the acceptable year of the Lord." Then He said, in effect: "That is My map of operations. That is the outline of My campaign. That is My social, political, and religious platform." There is not a great deal of doctrinal definition in that proclamation, but there is very much of philanthropic promise and purpose in it. That it would be more popular than a course in systematic theology, everybody can see. But that it contains more of the essence of religion than tons of discussion about doctrinal points is what the fewest Christians in nineteen centuries have been able to perceive. Yet this is just what Jesus understood His religion to mean.

One day a couple of messengers came from John the Baptist, who was in prison waiting for decapitation, to ask Jesus whether He was really the expected Messiah. The reply was very significant: "Go and show John again those things which ye do hear and see: the blind receive their sight, and the lame walk; the lepers are cleansed, and the deaf hear; the dead are raised up, and the poor have the Gospel preached unto them." In other words, Jesus said, "The undeniable proof that I am divine is not that I say so or that any one declares I am, but that I am doing a divine work, I am engaged in philanthropy." That is something of what Jesus understood His religion to mean.

Once Jesus was explaining the basis on which

final judgment would be pronounced upon mankind. That was a serious moment. It is very significant that on that solemn occasion Jesus said nothing about love to God, or public worship, or doctrinal standards. The whole matter was made to hinge on love to humanity. Persons who have fed the hungry, clothed the naked, and visited those who were sick and in prison, deploy to the right, in the pictorial representation which Jesus draws, and those who have neglected these obligations file off to the left, evidently aware of the perfect fitness of the recompense to their deserts. For Jesus says, "Inasmuch as ye did, or did not, do these things to the least of My brethren, ye did, or did not, do them to Me." Augustus Cæsar sat one whole day each year in a public place and received alms like a common mendicant. Sentimentalists might fancy that an edifying spectacle. But Jesus would have us understand that in every destitute person He is perpetually standing before the world to receive help and solace. That is what He understood His religion to mean.

In all these illustrations of Christ's conception of His own religion we discover that He places the supreme emphasis upon brotherly love, upon philanthropy, upon doing good to others. God is a Father, men are brothers. To love God is to love humanity. Genuine love will show itself in sympathetic and practical helpfulness. That spirit will determine where and how we shall live hereafter. That is the center and core of Christ's religion as He understood it.

9

We can see, therefore, how the sharp words of Professor Richard T. Ely can be true, when he says that, "A man who claims to be a Christian, and at the same time is not a philanthropist, is a liar and a hypocrite." And we can realize how a man with such social ideas as have been described in terms which Jesus employed might be a better Christian, though he never heard of Christ, than the man who has enveloped himself with the doctrines of Christianity as with a garment, but knows nothing of practical love for humanity.

In the solution of the problems of society it will be necessary to urge these principles in the teachings of Jesus upon the attention of all congregations of Christians, both for the illumination of the Church respecting its obligations, and for the enlightenment of the alienated people who misunderstand the position of the Church. The social message of Jesus bears distinctly upon both the accumulation and distribution of wealth, upon the duties as well as the rights of property-holders, and upon the mutual obligations of employer and employees alike. Future generations will ask concerning any rich philanthropist whose gifts have added distinction to his name and benefits to his fellows, not only, "What did he do with his money?" but also, "How and where did he get it?"

The larger conquests of our times seem to require vast sums of money, and the mad scramble for wealth which characterizes our day is not so much

a mark of avarice as it is a desire for power. Money
is the apparent wonder-worker of the age. Inordinately rich men seem to be demanded by the very
circumstances of our civilization. This is not the
actual truth. It is in no sense important that colossal fortunes should be reared. The man who is pushing through his day with a total disregard of the
higher interests of life, in order that he may accumu-
late vast wealth, may be pursuing his course with a
view to the ultimate filling of a great opportunity
to benefit his generation, but he is a misguided en-
thusiast. Enormous possessions by any man are not
required for the advantage of society. A whole
people lifted above the level of grinding necessity
would accomplish all that civilization requires without the aid of a single Crœsus. The great libraries
which are being scattered over our land by the munifi-
cence of our philanthropic iron-master, the universities which are being built through the generosity of
great capitalists, the museums of art, of natural history, and of antiquities, the hospitals, alms-houses,
asylums, homes for the relief of the unfortunate,
might all be constructed and equipped with the
people's money without the aid of a single millionaire.
The great cathedrals, the noble churches, the splendid
memorials to departed greatness and genius which
fittingly mark our country's advancement, could all
be reared by the united gifts of a competent people
without the interference of one financial magnate.
Let all the people be exalted in material conditions,

and let us all be permeated by the spirit of culture
and religion, and the monuments which their generosity and devotion shall rear will reflect far greater
glory upon the commonwealth than all those separate
contributions to the beauty and order of our times
which are made by the gifts of enormously wealthy
individuals.

If you were asked to name the finest memorial
of Egyptian greatness which survives the tooth of
time, you would with perfect propriety mention the
Pyramids. As Rawlinson says, "Nothing more perfect mechanically has ever been erected since that
time." It is not strange that travelers have invari-
ably experienced the strongest admiration for them.
The emotions of great men from Herodotus to
Napoleon have been stirred by the sight of them.
The Greeks and Romans regarded them as among
the seven wonders of the world, and even modern
writers have questioned if they could really be the
work of human hands. But these Pyramids are enduring memorials not only of Egypt's glory and
greatness, but also of her disgrace and shame. They
were erected at an almost incalculable cost of blood
and treasure. They are the product in large part
of the unrequited toil of slaves. Thousands of human
lives were sacrificed to make them possible. Is it
altogether certain that future generations will not
look upon some of our most splendid institutions
as evidences of a similar disregard of the value of
human life, when it is remembered that many of the

most impressive structures of our day were made
out of the insufficiently paid toil of humble artisans,
and were virtually dedicated to the glory of men
who had gained the mastery of thousands of human
beings, while they heaped up for themselves incalculable sums of money?

It is a mark of virtue in a man possessing power
that he refrains from using it for his selfish advantage, and it would redound to the glory of
America, and of the Christian Church which plays
so important a part in the life of the people, if
men with the ability to become millionaires would
have the courage to content themselves with smaller
accumulations in order that less capable persons might
be raised to a loftier level. It requires heroism for
one who knows he could become wealthy to turn aside
from the lure of fortune and devote himself to the
task of uplifting the millions of his fellow-beings
who do not possess his abilities, but how noble is
such self-denial! The wife of Hugh Price Hughes
declared that the greatest sacrifice of her distin-
guished husband was his willingness not to become a
great preacher. He might have attained this emi-
nence, but it would have been at the expense of his
effort for the poor. How much better than vast
accumulations in the hands of a few men would be
the strengthening of character, the diffusion of
brotherhood, and the general elevation of society,
achieved by the devotion of men of intellect, not to
the business of making fortunes, but to the humane

work of saving society! It is the present business
of the Church to teach her wealthy adherents the
beauty and power of this ideal.

Matthew Arnold said, years ago, "Our present
social inequality materializes the upper class, vul-
garizes the middle class, and brutalizes the lower
class." The most apposite commentary upon this
text is the current life of America. Organized Christianity has here an immense task upon its hands.
The social situation looms large and portentous before the Church. It is huge in bulk and wears a
frowning aspect. The pulpit has been first in giving
it cognizance, and the pew must be patient to hear
about it. But this is only the beginning. It may
be sentimentally beautiful, and practically true, to
say that the preaching of simple Gospel will ultimately solve all the questions which confront society,
but it is disgracefully indolent and crassly ignorant
to suppose that that blessed evangel, unaccompanied
by practical measures of relief for existing evils, will
ever settle our current discords. This is particularly obvious when we observe that those who are
most responsible for present social agitation are least
affected by the simple Gospel, since they hear it
most infrequently. What can the Church do in the
present situation? Its leaders can apply themselves
more seriously than they have done to the study of
the social situation; and this must be done, not
merely by the perusal of works on sociology, or of
books which have been written, either from the stand-

point of collectivism or of individualism, many of which totally, though perhaps unintentionally, misrepresent the current social crisis. Beyond and more important than all study of social doctrines must be a personal familiarity with the causes of the present social contention, obtained from an actual observation at close range of the conditions in our social organism. In all our theological seminaries there ought to be a department of practical or applied sociology, and connected with this department there should be a social or religious settlement in some adjacent city. Our ministers themselves should, as far as possible, secure a personal point of contact between themselves and the working people. They should know how they live; they should acquaint themselves with the peculiar limitations of their lives; they should ascertain their particular temptations; they should correct their misapprehensions regarding the real attitude of the Church; they should carry back to their congregations the knowledge thus acquired, and they should apply it fearlessly in their social teachings from the pulpit. Every public leader ought to be broad-minded enough to divest himself of any personal irritation which he may feel concerning the attitude of working people toward the Church, and discuss the subject of industrial reform on the basis of its fundamental principles. One may be exasperated at the disposition of the laboring people in our times to do as little work as possible, and to require for that service the largest compensation which can be wrung from the unwilling public. One may feel that in the present agitation organized labor is showing a desire to wield the terrors of despotism in as cruel a fashion as was ever manifested by the most soulless corporation. Nevertheless, he ought in the spirit of his Master to treat the general situation with statesmanlike impartiality. The social teachings of Jesus really constitute one of the largest elements in the legitimate utterances of the pulpit, and are so plain and so widely applicable that no student of the New Testament need be at loss concerning their meaning. Such a study will disclose the utter folly of indiscriminate assaults upon capital, employers, corporations, and trusts, as well as the wickedness of inconsiderate attacks upon organized labor. The modern preacher needs to ask divine help to save him from paroxysms of passion on either side of this great question. A cool analysis of the situation, a thoughtful exposition of the teachings of Jesus Christ as applied to both employer and employe, a constant proclamation of Christian ideals to meet the requirements of the present conflict—these are the indispensable requisites of a sane and successful ministry in these exacting times.

At all hazards, the Church must throw herself into the current social agitation, not as a reluctant laggard, but as the informing genius and the controlling mind of the movement which she has really inspired by her teachings. She must avail herself of the temper of the times. This is an age of great opulence, but also of impressive economies. Science has taught us how to extract wealth from by-products which formerly were regarded as worthless. We find fortunes in culm-piles, and princely riches in scrap-heaps. We are making a greater number of useful articles from petroleum than our Oriental neighbors get out of the palm-tree. We are learning each day new and cheaper processes of utilization. We are availing ourselves of natural forces in every possible way. We are laying hold upon every ounce of energy we can discover. We are trying to increase the efficiency of the human body by feeding man with the most nutritive and energy-producing foods we can devise. We are practicing physical culture and experimenting with all kinds of psychological artifices in order to conserve the forces of the human animal. All this is typical of the prevalent mood of society to increase its power. We are striving to redeem the waste of society by making the utmost of the feeble and the incompetent. Society is preparing to bear on its bosom the incapable until they become capable. This spirit of the age is interfering with the evolutionary process. It is antagonizing the law of the "survival of the fittest." It is insisting upon the survival of the unfit, and it does this with the consciousness that the social organism will ultimately reap an incalculable benefit. To be sure, there is a school of philosophers teaching a contrary doctrine. They are insisting that the deformed, the defective, and the diseased shall be ruthlessly exterminated. This would mean the annihilation of the incorrigibly criminal and vicious class. But a society pervaded by the humane spirit of our times shudders at such a remedy, whether applied to the redress of physical or of social ills. An intelligent woman asked the other day if the Spartan method of exposing the weak and incompetent to death would not, after all, produce in the long run a sturdier and worthier race than the method of our philanthropic age. Unquestionably we should by this means secure a brood of Titans, with muscles of brass and sinews of steel, great portentous figures, with brains and magnificent as Milton's "Lucifer," and possessed of wills as diabolic, men of intellectual prodigiousness, but as cold and unfeeling as Mont Blanc; magnificent brutes, ramping over the earth, building colossal monuments to power and selfishness, making a world in which poetry would suffocate, art would be devitalized, music would be starved into silence, its strings all broken by violence; eloquence would be quenched, religion frozen to death, and, the graces of civilization being obliterated, life would be an unspeakable calamity. The spirit of our times will not tolerate such a catastrophe. The Church of our times must prophesy and produce a golden era of kindliness and love, and by every practical agency labor to show itself, not merely in sympathy with the temper of the age, but eager to lead the hosts of men as rapidly as possible to the fulfillment of humanity's dream of universal peace, saying, with a modern poet.:

> " We live to hail the season
>   By gifted minds foretold,
>   When man shall live by reason,
>   And not alone for gold.
>   When man to man united,
>   And every wrong thing righted,
>   The whole world shall be lighted
>   As Eden was of old."